EASY UPGRADES>
KITCHENS

FROM THE EDITORS OF

CONTENTS

EASY UPGRADES: COLOR

IDEA FILE

A hit of color can turn the functional eleme
eye-catching focal points. Cabinets make
can play up or tone down with your choice
ceilings lend themselves to clever treatme
Here are more colorful ideas for transform

THE PERFECT KITCHEN

AMERICA'S TOP REMODELING RESOURCE for more than 30 years, *This Old House* has renovated dozens of kitchens with the TV cameras running and featured hundreds more in *This Old House* magazine and at thisoldhouse.com. Along the way, we've learned a lot about what works and what doesn't, where you should splurge and where you can save—and in *Easy Upgrades: Kitchens,* we're pleased to be able to share that knowledge with you.

Most people's complaints about their kitchens are similar: an awkward layout, poor foot-traffic flow, not enough counter space, too little storage, outmoded decor. On the pages that follow, you'll see how dozens of homeowners solved these real-world problems to create kitchens that are comfortable, functional, and stylish, too.

To figure out what kind of space is right for you, take a look at the sample **floor plans** up front for examples of classic ways to configure space for maximum safety,

comfort, and utility. Then start flipping through the **Before and After** case studies and the pages of kitchen **Idea Files.** In them, you'll find inspiration for projects of every type, from budget-minded redos to cooks' kitchens to family-friendly gathering places. Then begin to put it all together with the cabinetry, fixtures, finishes, and materials that are right for your style and your budget.

Throughout this book, you'll see **callouts** highlighting special design details, and boxes featuring **advice from *This Old House* pros** on how you can re-create the look you like in your own home. You'll also find two more categories of information: **Easy Upgrades** are great ideas you can adapt for any project, whether you're taking a room down to the studs or simply making cosmetic changes, while **Smart Saves** are expert strategies for cutting costs without cutting corners.

We know remodeling a kitchen can be stressful. There are more choices than ever,

callouts

Design details you can adapt for any project, no matter how big or small

easy upgrades

Simple ways to get high-end looks at a price you can afford

pro advice

Expert tips for getting the kitchen you want

floor plans

Creative layouts and solutions to common space-planning problems

and while new technologies can increase comfort, they often require more in the way of advance planning and complex construction. Then there's the mess and, of course, the expense—both of which can keep you up at night. After years of helping people improve their spaces, we're realistic enough to acknowledge that there will always be unanticipated hiccups along the way. But if you plan carefully, keep a close eye on your priorities, and invest in the highest quality materials your budget will bear, you'll end up with a space that delivers the pleasure you want and the performance modern life demands. In short, the perfect kitchen: The one that's right for you.

6 BASIC KITCHEN LAYOUTS

For all the many decisions that go into completing a successful kitchen renovation, your most important consideration should also be your first: an ideal layout. No doubt you've heard of the kitchen work triangle, a layout strategy that limits the distance between your sink, stove, and refrigerator for safety and convenience. Designers recommend the total distance between the triangle legs should be no more than 26 feet, but the arrangement can be manipulated in various ways to satisfy your cooking needs. The result should be a comfortable and efficient kitchen with plenty of storage just where you need it most.

To help determine the optimal layout for your kitchen, here are six prototypical floor plans. A variation of one of them is sure to be the perfect shape for your new cook space.

U-SHAPE

With three walls of counter space and storage, this arrangement provides a compact and efficient work area for a single chef. (By locating appliances carefully, two work areas can be created in each corner of the U to accommodate dual cooks.) Though not spacious enough for entertaining, the room can still handle a breakfast table separate from the cooking area. The best plan: Place the refrigerator and cooktop on opposite walls, with the sink centered in the base of the U.

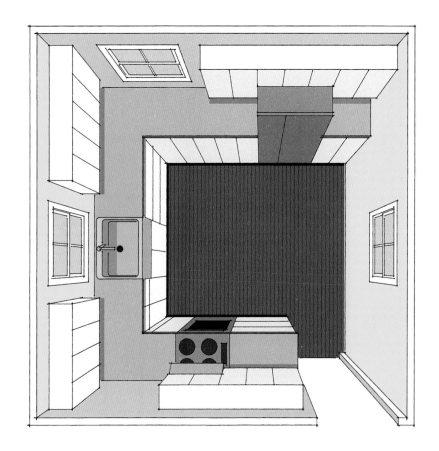

L-SHAPE

The beauty of this layout is how well it works within a limited space; in fact, its two legs use less space than a U-shaped kitchen while still providing a functional and efficient work zone for a single cook. The key is to avoid interrupting the corner of the L: The expanse of countertop should be unbroken. A refrigerator works well at one end when the sink and range are almost equidistant from its corner. There may even be room in the middle of the kitchen to fit a small table for casual family meals.

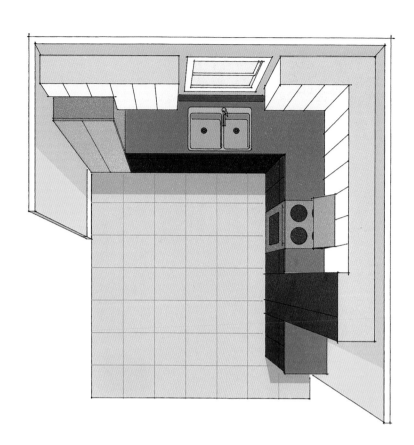

GALLEY

This layout offers maximum efficiency when there's not much space to work with. Its two parallel counters make all points of the work triangle equally accessible. One drawback to a galley is congestion, especially when doors to any appliance or cabinet are open. It's tough for more than two people to cook in this kitchen at the same time. To reduce congestion, make the center aisle 4 to 6 feet wide, and place the sink and refrigerator on one wall with the range on the opposite wall.

✳ TOH DESIGN ADVICE

Make a list of every activity you use your kitchen for, including the noncooking ones. This will help you plan the features and layout.

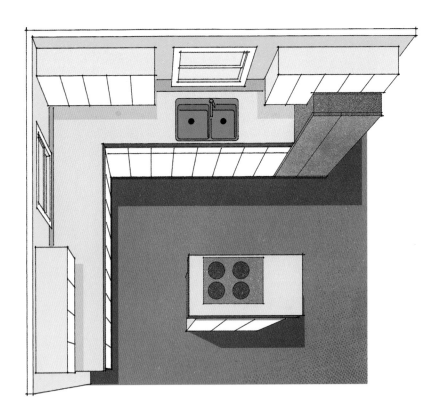

ISLAND
When space allows, adding a work island to a kitchen with an L- or U-shape will dramatically improve its function. The room instantly gains an additional countertop. Then, outfitted with either a cooktop or a second sink, the island offers another prep area and can even double as a breakfast bar. In an L- or U-shaped kitchen, provide aisles that are at least 36 inches wide—42 inches is better—around the island.

10 top kitchen-planning guidelines

Designing a kitchen is an art and a science. You'll improve your chances of success if you incorporate standard guidelines. Here are the most important:

1 For optimum clearance, allow 42 to 48 inches between cabinets or appliances that face each other.

2 In kitchens smaller than 150 square feet, try for at least 13 running feet of base cabinets, 12 feet of wall cabinets, and 11 feet of countertops. In kitchens 150 square feet or larger, go with at least 16 feet of base cabinets, 15½ feet of wall cabinets, and 16½ feet of countertops.

3 Allow 15 to 18 inches between upper and lower cabinetry.

4 For maximum convenience, leave at least 24 inches of counter space on one side of the sink and at least 18 inches on the other.

5 To create the most accessible landing for unloading groceries, provide at least 15 inches of counter space on the handle side of a standard refrigerator, or 15 inches on each side if it's a side-by-side or French-door model. Or create a landing area on an island or peninsula directly across from the refrigerator, but no more than 48 inches away.

6 For cleanup ease, install the dishwasher within 36 inches of one edge of the sink and provide at least 21 inches of standing room next to it.

7 Provide at least 15 inches of counter near the microwave for prep convenience.

8 To maximize storage, include at least one corner unit of cabinetry.

9 For comfort and better ergonomics, plan for work counters of different heights. Counters 28 to 32 inches off the floor may be easiest for chopping and seated use; those 36 to 45 inches off the floor are best for general tasks. Higher counters accommodate taller cooks.

10 When placing a cabinet above the cooktop, provide at least 24 inches of clearance to a fireproof surface and 30 inches to a flammable surface.

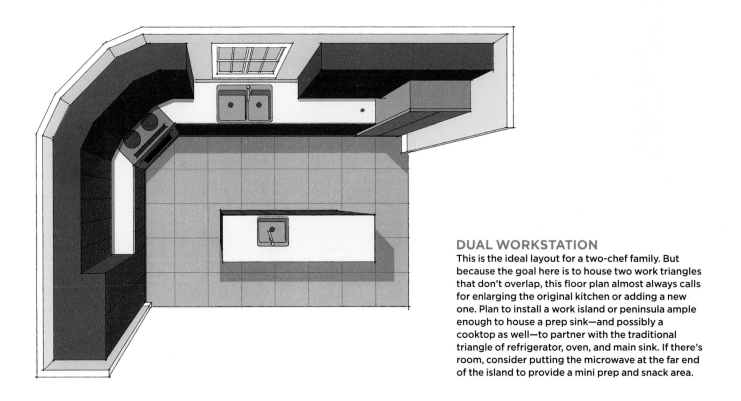

DUAL WORKSTATION

This is the ideal layout for a two-chef family. But because the goal here is to house two work triangles that don't overlap, this floor plan almost always calls for enlarging the original kitchen or adding a new one. Plan to install a work island or peninsula ample enough to house a prep sink—and possibly a cooktop as well—to partner with the traditional triangle of refrigerator, oven, and main sink. If there's room, consider putting the microwave at the far end of the island to provide a mini prep and snack area.

WORK CENTER

This relatively new approach creates discrete areas for food preparation, cooking, and cleanup. Like the dual-workstation kitchen (above), the arrangement is great for multiple cooks and requires the same enlarged dimensions. Use the island as the prep area, and link the refrigerator and other food storage (including an under-counter refrigerator or freezer drawers) to the prep sink and a chopping block. The cooking zone centers around the cooktop and should be outfitted with storage for pots, pans, utensils, cookbooks, herbs, and spices. Wall ovens for baking can occupy a separate corner. To provide a cleanup area, place the main sink, dishwasher, and storage for the dishes, glasses, and flatware nearby.

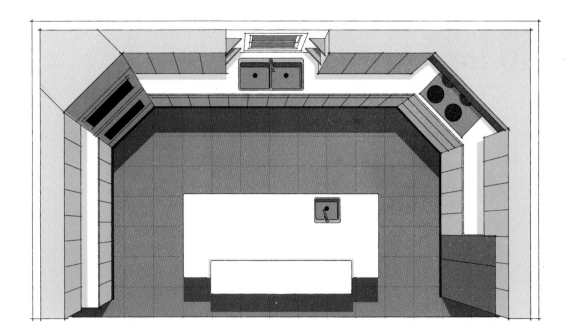

A CENTER ISLAND serves as prep area, gathering place, and cookie-making station. This one is topped with mahogany finished with a food-grade oil. An overhang allows stools to be pulled up for snacking.

CHAPTER 1>

THE FAMILY KITCHEN

It is referred to as the heart of the home for good reason. The kitchen is where the action is, and not just for those three squares a day. There's snack time, homework time, and just general hanging-out-with-mom-and-dad time. A layout with a center island creates a natural come-together place. One with an open plan that has few interior walls lets parents keep an eye on kids' comings and goings while easing traffic flow. Take a look at the examples on the following pages to see how to create a kitchen that will keep the family close.

before +afters

The last redo, circa 1970, had a poorly designed layout with lots of wasted space. The prep area was pushed to the perimeter, leaving a dead zone in the middle.

before

ONE ROOM, MANY USES

PROBLEM> While large, the U-shaped layout was inefficient and ultimately inhospitable.
SOLUTION> Reconfigure the space, add an island, and carve out nooks for the computer and crafts.

KITCHENS ARE NATURAL GATHERING PLACES, and the more they cue up feelings of hearth and home, the stronger the pull. But previous redos of this 1906 Shingle-style house's kitchen left all the workstations on the perimeter and nothing in the middle. The sterile layout discouraged the owners and their young daughter from grabbing a meal together, working on hobbies, or catching up on paperwork. They hoped a rethinking of the kitchen could yield a single open space, where three people could spend time on separate projects together.

So they hired an architect to help them arrive at a design that would satisfy all their needs, which included connecting the kitchen to a new family room. She recommended bumping out the back wall a few feet, squaring off the kitchen, and making space for two alcoves. This in effect yielded three rooms in one, with a computer desk and a crafts center beside the cooking area. Opening up the old sink wall connected the kitchen to the addition, with a two-sided hutch serving as a room divider. Introducing a 1930s Wedgewood stove that the wife scored in an online auction sealed the marriage between modern efficiency and vintage styling. The once yawning room is now cozy—and busy as a beehive.

after

Side-by-side alcoves accommodate a computer station and a crafts area in this multipurpose family space. The salvaged wood hutch and island maintain its turn-of-the-century feel.

When two faucets are in close proximity, keep the style the same for a finished look.

THE UPPER AND LOWER CABINETS have Shaker-style doors, while beadboard covers the small pantry units lining the top, as well as the backsplash.

An under-counter microwave lets kids help themselves at snacktime. →

AFTER

Bumping out the back wall squared off the room, allowing for office and crafts areas. An island now anchors the cook space. With the fridge tucked into a niche stolen from the living room, a hutch adds storage lost when the old sink wall came down to create a large opening to a new family room.

the plan

BEFORE

The kitchen was interrupted by three doorways that shoved all the work stations to the perimeter.

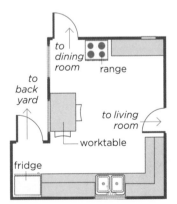

to dining room
range
to back yard
to living room
worktable
fridge

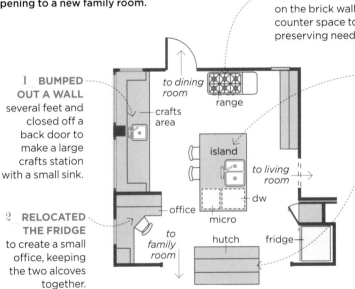

to dining room
crafts area
range
island
to living room
office
micro
to family room
hutch
fridge
dw

1 BUMPED OUT A WALL several feet and closed off a back door to make a large crafts station with a small sink.

2 RELOCATED THE FRIDGE to create a small office, keeping the two alcoves together.

3 INSTALLED A VINTAGE STOVE on the brick wall, and shifted the counter space to an adjacent wall, preserving needed landing space.

4 PUT IN AN ISLAND to gain more prep space as well as a gathering spot for family meals and activities.

5 REMOVED MOST OF THE SINK WALL to open the kitchen to the new family room, adding back storage with a two-sided hutch.

the details

→ **THE HOME OFFICE** finds its niche in an alcove, with the crafts station on the other side of the partition wall. Both alcoves have a lowered ceiling to separate them from the kitchen even as they remain open to it.

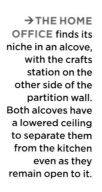

↓ **THE TWO-SIDED HUTCH** acts as a divider between the kitchen and the new family-room addition.

EASY UPGRADE

To adapt an existing hutch as a room divider, finish the raw side. Even better, add open shelves. You don't want the cupboard to turn its back on either room.

→ **A SECOND SINK** in the crafts area is paired with a gooseneck faucet to accommodate tall buckets and vases.

← **UPDATED STORAGE** includes roll-out shelves. The ones here allow everyone easy access to art supplies.

Tools hung from hooks are easy to access and keep the counter clear.

A poor layout and dated materials made preparing meals a chore and crowded everyone out of the space except the cook.

IMPROVE THE FLOW

PROBLEM> Its awkward layout turned a vintage kitchen into a clutter magnet. SOLUTION> Consolidate workstations and bump up the square footage to accommodate a variety of family activities.

A GOOD REMODEL OFTEN PAYS HOMAGE to the past while functioning very much in the present. This 1920s house, while long on vintage charm, fell short in the kitchen: a bare-bones box with a speckled linoleum floor, tile counters, and an isolated eating nook. To create an airy gathering space that would open to the adjoining family room, an exterior wall was bumped out a few feet and two interior walls were taken down, combining the former kitchen and a laundry area into one large rectangular space.

Now, a center cooking island allows mom to keep an eye on the kids. Fridge, wine cooler, and a food pantry are lined up in a freestanding cabinetry unit that separates the kitchen and family room in the open plan. Clean-lined, no-frills cabinet boxes, many with open shelves, take the place of standard uppers, and long runs of volcanic-stone counters have a subtle, natural look. A sculptural range hood hangs from the rafters, and a larger window by the eating nook brings the outdoors inside. The kitchen's deconstructed footprint and sleek appliances have a contemporary feeling while its soft palette hints at the home's vintage origins. The result: an easy-going family hub that streamlines daily life.

after

Fresh colors, an open plan with an integrated eating nook, and distinct areas for storage and prep make an inviting space for both cook and kids.

THE CENTER ISLAND, topped with a vent hood, is the kitchen's command center.

the plan

AFTER
Bumping out the back wall and eliminating two others created one large room with more space for prep and family members.

BEFORE
The closed-off kitchen was awkward to navigate, with a dead-end eating nook.

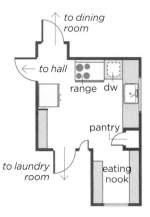

1 **REPLACED A WALL** with a unit that divides the kitchen and family room. It holds fridge, pantry, and cookbooks on one side, media equipment on the other.

2 **ANNEXED THE LAUNDRY ROOM** to gain a more workable rectangular space and a wide opening to the family room.

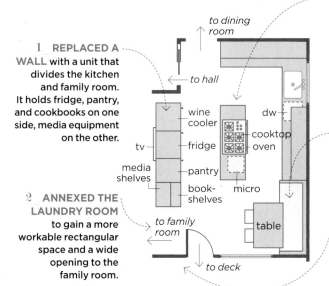

3 **ADDED AN ISLAND** that brings together the cooktop, oven, and microwave, plus prep space, minimizing collisions among cooks, sous-chefs, and table setters.

4 **BUILT IN A BANQUETTE** and table for an open eating nook just steps from the cooking and cleanup areas.

5 **BUMPED OUT** the back wall a few feet to capture even more square footage.

↓ SOFT BLUE and crisp green add contrast and depth to open shelves.

← OPEN CABINETS keep daily-use items close by and maintain the room's airy feeling

EASY UPGRADE

Install oversize bar pulls on simple cabinet doors to play up their sleek look. They are easy to grab and do double duty as a place to tuck a dish towel.

↑ A CUSTOM CUTTING BOARD overlaps countertop edges for stability but can be moved around easily.

A lamp plugged into an outlet by the banquette lights the table for homework. ↓

← THE EATING NOOK includes family-friendly, wipe-clean fabrics on the banquette cushions, a birch-veneer table that ceramic plates won't scratch, and an outlet to plug in a laptop.

↑ THE ISLAND holds all cooking functions plus pots and pans; a kid-height convection-microwave can be accessed behind the flip-up door.

Charcoal grout doesn't show stains and gives subway tile a warm, aged look.

before

A previous redo left beige tile floors and laminate doors in a space that could not fit all the members of the family at the same time.

SQUEEZE IN AN ISLAND

PROBLEM> Cramped and outdated, the space was too tight for a family of six.
SOLUTION> Rearrange the appliances and create task-focused areas that can handle food prep, meals, and the steady patter of little feet.

THE KITCHEN CAN PLAY A PIVOTAL ROLE in the "move or improve" debate. It certainly did here. While the homeowners loved the architecture of their 1920s Tudor Revival—think black-and-white-marble foyer, leaded-glass windows, paneled oak doors—just five years after moving in, they were considering selling. With four young kids in the mix, navigating the room's dysfunctional layout was making daily living a chore. There was minimal counter space, the fridge door blocked the entryway, and worse, a drafty, unheated pantry closet made the space uncomfortable in winter.

Ultimately the couple turned to a professional kitchen designer to help them reimagine the space. Together they discovered that by cutting back a wall leading to the rear staircase and removing the pantry, they could gain 6 square feet for a new layout that included a center island and a more open connection to the eating area. Creamy subway tile with charcoal grout, custard glass schoolhouse lights, a farm sink, and dark cabinetry created a period style in sync with the house. Now traffic flows more easily for the busy household, there's more counter and storage space, and the center island brings the family together for snacks and conversation.

after

Now the kitchen has a period look that suits the Tudor-style house and a floor plan that handles the many activities of a busy young family.

THE FAMILY KITCHEN
> SQUEEZE IN AN ISLAND

→ BLACK X-FRONT CABINETS
with opaque ribbed-glass panels nod to the house's black-and-white-marble foyer and distinguish a desk area that doubles as a bar.

↓ CHALKBOARD FRIDGE PANELS
hide fingerprints and show off doodles. The same wall holds the microwave, cookbooks, and small appliances.

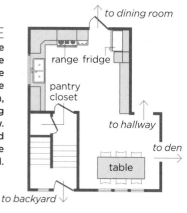

Wood floors help muffle the noise of little feet running to and fro. →

the plan

BEFORE
The fridge and range flanked the door to the dining room, impeding traffic flow. Prep and storage space were minimal.

to dining room ↑

range fridge

pantry closet

to hallway ↑

to den →

table

to backyard ↓

AFTER
Annexing the pantry closet and cutting back the wall opposite it allowed for an island and reconfiguring of the appliances.

1 **MOVED THE FRIDGE** to where the range had been, so it's now just steps from the sink.

2 **REMOVED THE PANTRY CLOSET** to create a new home for the range.

3 **CREATED A NEW PANTRY** with floor-to-ceiling cabinets. The long counter next to it acts as a desk and doubles as a bar when the couple entertains.

4 **ADDED AN ISLAND** to gain more prep space as well as a family gathering spot.

5 **CUT BACK THE WALL** opposite the old pantry for a better connection with the eating area.

to dining room ↑

micro

fridge pantry

desk/bar

dw

range island

to hallway

to office

table

to backyard ↓

the details

↓ **LIBRARY LAMPS** provide over-the-sink task lighting and coordinate with other bronze fixtures in the room.

← **WHITE TRIM AND BEIGE WALLS** make the opened-up dining space feel light and bright. New windows and oak floors blend with those in the rest of the house.

↑ **A TILE BORDER** made of stone mosaic lines the wall behind the desk; it coordinates with a geometric accent along the range wall.

→ **A SLIVER OF WHITE GRANITE** to the left of the range gives the cook elbow room and a splatter-proof area to stow frequently used cooking oils and condiments.

↑ **A BUILT-IN BENCH** in the eating area helps streamline the space and corrals the kids for family dinners.

EASY UPGRADE

A small recess at the bottom of a banquette protects it from scuff marks.

The hodgepodge kitchen had only two keepers: the range and the fridge.

SWAP SPACES

PROBLEM> The minimal, awkwardly arranged space had poor flow and function.
SOLUTION> Flopping the kitchen with the family room allowed for an expanded footprint and a more comfortable, light-filled hangout.

WHEN TWO PEOPLE UNDERTAKE A MAJOR REDO, some negotiating is required. The owners of this 1909 house in Seattle shared a vision of a colorful kitchen opening onto a porch. But the husband wanted a wood floor and cabinets with clear glass fronts, while the wife wanted no-fuss flooring and less transparency for the hardworking family hub. Pale linoleum and seeded glass proved to be the right compromise.

There was no hesitation on either side, however, when their designer suggested an easy way to gain more space: Have the kitchen and the family room trade places. Details like the coffered ceiling and arches trimmed to match ones on the porch make the brand-new space feel like it has a heritage. And features like two long runs of countertop on opposite walls mean there's plenty of room for a pair of cooks in the kitchen with teenage daughters lending a hand at the center island. The couple seized the opportunity that a complete remodel offers to treat themselves to amenities, of course, including a gas line threaded outside to feed a grill. The redo's success is one thing everyone agrees on.

after

Now in a new spot, the kitchen is larger and more hospitable to a variety of activities for the whole gang.

Cabinet tops double as display space for an array of colorful vintage bottles.
↓

THE FAMILY KITCHEN
> SWAP SPACES

→ **THE EXISTING RANGE AND HOOD** are now complemented by soapstone countertops, creamy subway tiles, and upper cabinets neatly finished with a display shelf and seeded-glass panels.

↓ **THE ORNAMENTED ARCH** over the eating nook repeats porch details and frames a view of the dining room's coffered ceiling.

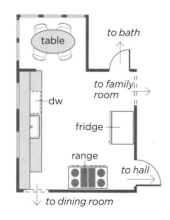

the plan

BEFORE
The kitchen had room for a dining table but lacked sufficient storage, prep space, and style.

table

to bath

dw

to family room

fridge

range

to hall

to dining room

AFTER
Relocated to the larger family room and joined to a porch, the expanded space is sunnier and big enough for an eating nook, an island—and a steady flow of family and friends.

1 **SWAPPED PLACES** with the family room and annexed part of the hall to gain light, space, and porch access.

2 **PUT AN ISLAND** at the center for food prep, meals on the go, and socializing.

3 **ADDED OVERSIZE WINDOWS,** a sliding glass door, and a top row of leaded panes to bring in lots of natural light, even in winter.

4 **FLANKED THE RANGE** with countertops and cabinets for lots more storage and prep space.

5 **BUILT IN AN EATING NOOK** and a pantry for better flow and function.

to porch

dw

micro

fridge

range

island

to family room

open shelves

table

to hall

pantry

the details

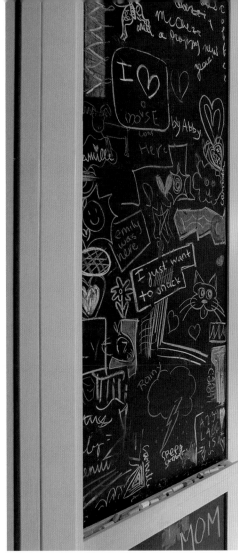

→ **A MAGNETIC CHALKBOARD** near the entry to the family room serves as a scribble pad and message center.

↑ **THE WALNUT-TOPPED ISLAND** holds cookbook shelves on one side and a microwave on the other. The shelves are slightly recessed, so stools tuck out of the way of foot traffic when not in use.

EASY UPGRADE

Open storage on the wide side of an island creates a convenient catchall. Opt for adjustable shelves that let you customize cubbies to conform to changing needs.

→ **OIL-RUBBED BRONZE** hinges, latches, and pulls evoke vintage kitchens; oversize subway tiles freshen the look.

↑ **A COFFERED CEILING** was built by boxing out and trimming beams for a Craftsman-style effect. Can lights are imperceptible until switched on.

South- and west-facing garage walls were perfect for windows that would flood the kitchen with natural light. *before*

CONVERT A BLANK SLATE

PROBLEM> The existing galley kitchen couldn't fit the large family, let alone their friends.
SOLUTION> Take over the unfinished garage to create an open, friendly space with plenty of windows, workstations, and places to gather.

FEAR THAT THE FAMILY DINNER IS NEARLY EXTINCT? Take heart. In this sunny, welcoming kitchen, the homeowners and their four children gather five nights a week for an evening meal—and their neighbors have a standing invitation to join them. "If they like the smell of what's cooking, I hope they'll come over," says the wife, whose priority was a space that could comfortably seat eight to 10. To accommodate a large table and room for the kids to snack and do homework, the family needed to upgrade the galley-style kitchen that came with their Cape Cod home.

With no room to expand the space, they chose to relocate it, taking over the two-car garage. With its south- and west-facing exterior walls, it was a natural to become a light, bright gathering place. The designer relegated the work zone to two adjoining walls, adding an island big enough to host prep work and homework. The couple got the not-so-new look they were after with glazed, cream-colored cabinets and a stamped-metal backsplash that evokes old tin ceilings—exactly the kind of family-centered, timeless-looking kitchen they wanted.

The kids can gather around the 9-foot-long island, which is topped with granite. The tin-ceiling-panel backsplash was aged with faux painting, then clear-coated for easy cleaning. *after*

True divided-light windows offer a view and echo the paneling on the cabinets →

Make it kid-friendly

TIPS FROM
COLETTE SCANLON,
TOH DESIGN EDITOR

1 **Open up the layout.** Fewer walls and clear sight lines mean you can always keep the kids in view and vice versa. Take advantage of an open plan by dotting it with places for kids (and their friends) to plant themselves, like an island or a peninsula.

2 **Create work stations.** Assign tasks such as cooking or cleaning in one area, to avoid traffic jams. Give the kids their own spot, such as a snack station with a small fridge and cupboard.

3 **Allow plenty of gathering places.** Offer more than one location for family to come together. In addition to an island, provide room for a good-size dining table or countertop run that can handle school projects or craft nights as well as weekday meals.

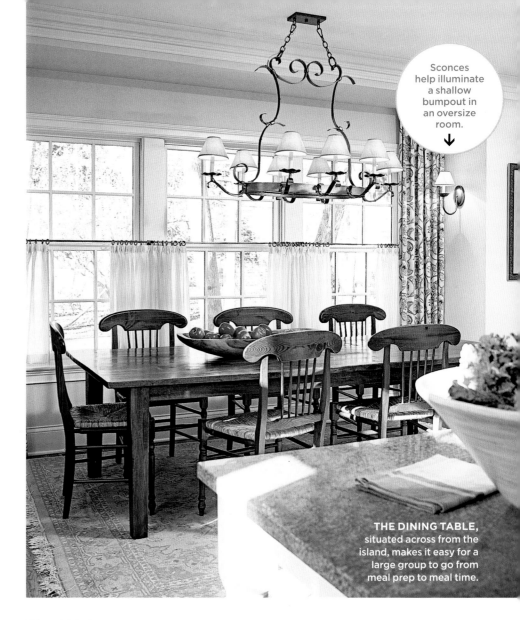

Sconces help illuminate a shallow bumpout in an oversize room. ↓

THE DINING TABLE, situated across from the island, makes it easy for a large group to go from meal prep to meal time.

the plan

BEFORE
The unfinished garage space was ripe for a remodel.

to office →

garage

AFTER
At the heart of the new kitchen is a long island that handles food prep and snack time. The table is tucked in a bumpout where the old garage doors had been.

1 **PUT IN A LARGE CENTRAL ISLAND** big enough for both prep and meals. A sink on the range side defines the work zone; the other side is open for tuck-under stool seating.

2 **BUMPED OUT A FEW FEET** on the wall that had held the garage doors to create a dining nook. Windows here and over the sink capture natural light.

3 **DOUBLED UP ON APPLIANCES** to meet the needs of a crowd. Two dishwashers and an extra oven do the job.

4 **CREATED A KIDS' SNACK AREA** in a cabinet with pull-out shelves. Placing it on the periphery keeps traffic out of the cook's way.

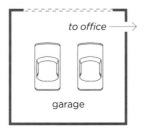

hutch

table

to pantry

to computer room

dw

dw

island

prep sink

oven/micro/tray storage

range · fridge

to family room

snack cabinet

the details

↓ **BUILT-IN STORAGE** for large serving pieces was inspired by old-fashioned plate racks. Partitions inside the cabinet keep platters and trays separate.

← **THE BACKSPLASH** is made of stamped sheet metal with medallion-motif panels inset above the cooktop. A decorative painter brushed on a faux-rust finish, applied metallic paint with a steel-wool pad to tone down the remaining silvery shine, then sealed it with polyurethane for easy cleanup.

EASY UPGRADE

Add a combination of dentil and crown moldings to dress up cabinet tops. Fancy flourishes like these look best with raised-panel doors.

↑ **BIRDCAGE-STYLE PULLS** in forged iron echo those found in archival photos of kitchens from the 1800s.

↑ **TURNED WOOD POSTS** flank the double-bowl sink and the island's snack bar to give the cabinetry a furniture look. Twin dishwashers, located on either side of the main sink, are hidden behind cabinet panels.

↑ **UNDER-CABINET TASK LIGHTING** shines halogen bulbs on countertops and illuminates the tin backsplash and creamy-green granite, as well as the homeowners' decorative pieces.

CHAPTER 2 >
THE BUDGET KITCHEN

It's the rare remodel where money is no object. For most of us, creating a realistic budget—and sticking to it—is key to getting the job done. But that doesn't mean you have to settle for a look that's basic or boring. Keep to the footprint if you can; minimizing construction costs means you'll have more to spend on things that show. Then think creatively with materials: Paint, salvage, and even closeouts can yield beautiful, stylish results. Read on for examples that will inspire your own thrifty ingenuity.

before
+afters

1_ **Keep the Layout**

2_ **Diner-Inspired**

3_ **Charm on the Cheap**

4_ **Idea File**

Dingy vinyl floors, yellow laminate counters, and dark cabinets made this 1970s kitchen feel dated and gloomy.

before

KEEP THE LAYOUT

PROBLEM> The dated space was dark and depressing, but there was no money for a gut reno.
SOLUTION> Work with what's there, shop for bargains and quality secondhand stuff, and invest plenty of sweat equity.

IT'S A COMMON KITCHEN-RENOVATION QUANDARY: How to afford stainless steel and stone on an almond-bisque-and-laminate budget? The answer for these homeowners lay in a straightforward approach: preserve elements of the existing kitchen that were still in good shape, cut labor costs by doing virtually all the work themselves, and shop sales and online classifieds for both new and used showpieces.

They were just being realistic. "To stay within the $6,000 we allotted for the project, gutting the whole kitchen was not an option," says the wife. By keeping the basic layout—with some minor tweaks—and painting the stained cabinets rather than replacing them, the couple was able to save big right off the bat. A carpentry course the husband took at a local community center provided him with DIY skills he later put to the test. For her part, the wife trolled the Internet and roamed the aisles of big-box stores in search of well-priced replacements for their tired appliances, harvest-gold vinyl floor, and yellow laminate countertops. Her first find was a year-old stainless-steel range, scored online for a third of its original price. The next biggie: granite countertops from a warehouse club. "The truth is, you just have to know where to look," says the sticker-savvy wife. "See those glass canisters by the sink? Only five bucks."

after

New bamboo floors, granite counters, and crisp white paint on the cabinets make the renovated kitchen look like a million bucks.

Beadboard and trim turn the existing soffit into a decorative feature.
↓

It took trips to three home centers to find enough sale-bin knobs and pulls for the room.
←

GROCERIES   TO DO

Get the goods cheap

TIPS FROM
COLETTE
SCANLON,
TOH DESIGN
EDITOR

1 **Eliminate shipping costs.** Search regional online classifieds for large items that you can pick up yourself to save on postal charges. For instance, it can cost as much as $200 to deliver a range bought from an out-of-state seller, versus the cost of gas if you buy locally.

2 **Use coupons and rebates.** Clip coupons from the Sunday paper. And sign up for e-mail blasts from stores you frequent. (Be selective or before you know it your inbox will be full of newsletters touting sales.) Some websites also aggregate and broadcast discounts via e-mail alerts that you can subscribe to.

3 **Compare prices.** If you find a deal through an online discount site, cross-check it with the manufacturer's retail price to make sure it's sufficiently reduced.

4 **Automate the auction.** If you're bidding on an online auction site, sign up for alerts that you've been outbid. Then you can log back on and up the ante.

5 **Sign up for credit-card points.** Make big purchases with your credit card to earn reward points that can be redeemed for gift cards from a wide array of stores. Just be sure to pay off the balance before the interest kicks in.

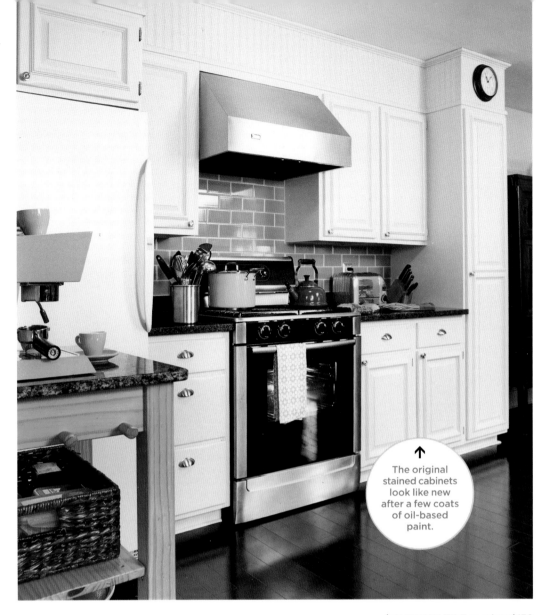

The original stained cabinets look like new after a few coats of oil-based paint.

↑ **SUBWAY TILE** cost just $136 for 20 square feet from a large home-supply store. The husband saved another $450 by doing the installation himself.

the plan

BEFORE + AFTER

A narrow path between the peninsula and the pantry was hard to navigate with the pantry door open. Shifting the pantry farther down the range wall eased traffic flow.

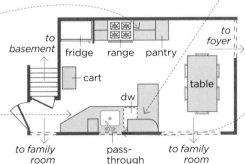

1 **BUILT AN UPPER AND BASE CABINET** for extra storage and counter space.

2 **EASED THE PASSAGE** to the family room by exchanging a sharply clipped corner for a longer, gentler angle.

3 **REMOVED CEILING-HUNG CABINETS** over the peninsula that obstructed the view of the dining area. Made two new cabinets with reeded-glass doors to fill the leftover void and to replace an odd-size one on the sink wall.

4 **MADE THE PASS-THROUGH PRACTICAL** by adding a wide granite ledge for serving up snacks to family or company in the adjacent family room.

the details

← **GRANITE COUNTERS** were a splurge, but a rebate lessened the blow. The sink was bought with a gift card acquired by cashing in credit-card reward points.

EASY UPGRADE

Swap out solid panels on a couple of upper cabinets for reeded glass. It lightens up the kitchen without putting cabinet contents totally on display.

↓ **THE TALL PANTRY CABINET** moved a few feet down the range wall so the door wouldn't open out toward the tip of the peninsula and block traffic.

↑ **THE WOOD DUTCH DOOR,** just $50 from an online classified ad, got a paint makeover. By leaving the top portion open, the homeowner can be in his office and keep an eye on the kids in the kitchen.

← **OPEN ACCESS** to the dining area allows the cook to stay involved with activity at the table and to pass plates across the peninsula. The chandelier was from an online retailer's clearance annex.

← **THE GRANITE-TOPPED CART** was just $75 from an online classified ad. The sleek flooring beneath it—375 square feet of ebonized bamboo—was left over from a local job site. At $750, it cost half the price of ordering the boards directly from the maker.

Gold laminate, dull brown cabinets, and a mottled mustard floor made the kitchen feel dismal. **before**

DINER-INSPIRED

PROBLEM> **A dingy and cramped 1960s remodel made the kitchen a poor fit for this 1920s home.** SOLUTION> **Take a cue from the streamlined, nonsense approach of Depression-era design, and put the family to work.**

THE OWNERS OF THIS VINTAGE HOUSE were taken with its solid construction and period details. The charm fell short in the kitchen, however, due to a late-1960s renovation that never addressed the utility of the space. Determining that they could give the kitchen more character and function, as well as space for a family-size table, the couple hired a carpenter to knock out a dividing wall and enclose a small back porch. While not adding significant square footage, the bumpout opened up the room to allow for that much-wanted dining table.

To trim costs, they did a lot of the work themselves, but turned to a pro for tasks they couldn't handle on their own, such as building cabinetry. They did manage to hang the cabinets themselves, enlisting the free labor of their children, who participated throughout the process, even weighing in on the choice of a floor. To keep daily maintenance of the kitchen to a minimum, the family opted for commercial vinyl tile, along with quartz counters that don't need sealing and wood windows that are low-maintenance aluminum on the outside. Resourceful bargain hunting also corralled the budget: The Formica table was scored for $10 from the online classifieds, and the chairs from a surplus school-supplies depot for about a buck apiece. It all came together in the end. Some visitors are even convinced the kitchen is original to the house!

after

Slightly bigger, the redone space hosts a diner-style table for six that can be moved as needed. Art Deco pendants keep the kitchen bright at night.

Using a pair of pendants that are similar but not the same adds an extra level of detail. →

↑ A SOFT COLOR SCHEME belies the kitchen's hard-wearing surface materials, while the addition of a door to the backyard handles the comings and goings of a busy family.

the plan

AFTER
Annexing a back porch created a more workable layout; adding windows brightened the space.

1 OPENED UP THE BREAKFAST NOOK by removing a dividing wall and annexing the porch. This allowed for a longer run of cabinets and countertops.

2 FREED UP THE RANGE, which had been jammed in a corner, by moving it to the other side of the dining-room door.

3 SQUARED OFF THE ROOM by bumping out an exterior wall where the back porch had stood, making way for a bigger table. Relocated the back door, swapped it for one with a stained-glass panel, and added two more windows to channel natural light into the space and enlarge the view.

4 CREATED A FRIDGE NICHE with a pullout pantry on one side and cabinets arranged hutch-style on the other.

BEFORE
The kitchen was too small to hold a family-size table and too dark for comfort.

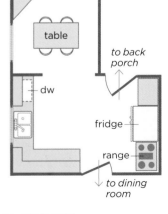

the details

↓ **A PULLOUT PANTRY** organizes bulky cans and boxes and helps to form a sleek niche for the fridge.

← **TO-THE-CEILING CABINETS** finished with white acrylic enamel lend a period look. Soft-green walls echo square vinyl tiles that compose the floor pattern, as well as slim green accent tiles paired with black dots and trim in the backsplash.

→ **A HUTCH-LIKE ASSEMBLY** of paneled lower units and upper cabinets with wavy-glass fronts shows off a cheerful collection of vintage Jadite. Chrome drawer pulls with black ridges coordinate with plain black knobs on doors.

↑ **EASY-CARE SURFACES** include matte-white ceramic tile, engineered quartz, and a sink with an integral drain board.

EASY UPGRADE

If cleanup is a concern, opt for a single-stem or wall-mount faucet—it will make tidying up the countertop behind the sink a cinch.

✳ TOH DESIGN ADVICE

Mix high- and low-end materials, like custom cabinets with vinyl floors, to rein in your overall cash outlay.

LE JARDIN
DE LA MAISON

White appliances blend into white cabinets, → saving the cost of expensive panels.

before

The existing kitchen had worn cabinets, pink-and-white laminate, and an acoustic-tile ceiling.

CHARM ON THE CHEAP

PROBLEM> The outdated kitchen was big but dreary, and the redo budget was small.
SOLUTION> Reuse some cabinets, customize the rest, and make a big design statement with low-cost materials.

TRY RENOVATING ON A BUDGET and see if you don't end up trimming a bit here and there until the best details are gone. Unless, of course, you take a page from the designer of this kitchen, who would rather sacrifice a few big-ticket items than a dozen smaller ones. "This was the least expensive project that I've ever done," the interior designer says of the space she conjured for friends, "and yet it's one of my favorites."

With the couple eager to shave costs—while gaining function and a home office—the designer rejected an apron sink, granite countertops, and stainless steel in favor of a white porcelain drop-in basin, lots of black laminate, and basic white workhorse appliances. These and other trade-offs afforded the couple custom built-ins and a hardworking island. Base cabinets were replaced to get needed drawer space, but the uppers simply got new doors and hardware. Blue paint cheers up the room, and a black-and-white vinyl checkerboard on the floor energizes the space. Molding adds a finished look while hiding signs of a former drop ceiling. Splurges include the beefy butcher-block top on the island and a vintage-style weighted work-light pendant that's a focal point over the sink, right where everyone can see it. The lesson, says the designer: "Put your money where it counts."

after

A dramatic checkerboard floor, blue paint, and vintage-style details add personality; more prep and storage space step up the function.

The contrast of blue walls with white trim and cabinets visually balances the checkerboard. →

↑ **THE OFFICE BUILT-IN** has "flipper" doors that keep the computer desk under wraps when not in use.

AFTER
Removing the partition wall allowed for a work island and created a more open space.

the plan

BEFORE
A partition wall split the space, and a drop ceiling made it feel cramped.

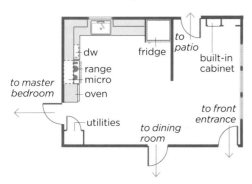

dw
fridge
range
micro
oven
to master bedroom
utilities
built-in cabinet
to patio
to dining room
to front entrance

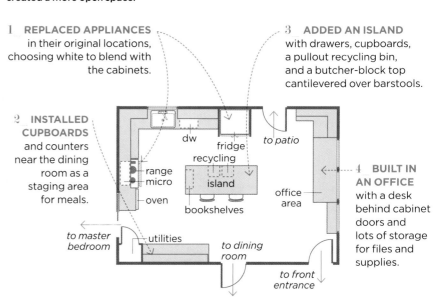

1 **REPLACED APPLIANCES** in their original locations, choosing white to blend with the cabinets.

2 **INSTALLED CUPBOARDS** and counters near the dining room as a staging area for meals.

3 **ADDED AN ISLAND** with drawers, cupboards, a pullout recycling bin, and a butcher-block top cantilevered over barstools.

4 **BUILT IN AN OFFICE** with a desk behind cabinet doors and lots of storage for files and supplies.

dw
fridge
recycling
range
micro
oven
island
bookshelves
office area
to patio
to master bedroom
utilities
to dining room
to front entrance

the details

↓ **THE L-SHAPED OFFICE BUILT-IN** keeps assorted craft supplies well organized.

← **A BEVELED EDGE** dresses up simple black laminate countertops. Trays slide into "found space" between two cabinets near the sink.

SMART SAVE

Mixing hardware styles—such as bin and bar pulls in the same finish, with faceted glass knobs—lends vintage charm to kitchen cabinets. It also allows you to make use of small lots of sale finds.

↑ **OPEN SHELVES** help tap every cubic inch of an island with a hardworking maple butcher-block countertop and furniture-like feet.

← **THE SPICE DRAWER** near the range has angled dividers to make finding the cinnamon as easy as pie.

IDEA FILE

Nobody wants to settle for a cookie-cutter cook space. But these days we're all looking to get more for, well, less. Here's how to use fresh paint and paper, vintage finds, and other smart buys to get made-to-order looks at off-the-shelf prices.

→ CREATE CRISP COTTAGE STYLE

1 HIGH PLATE RAIL. A deep shelf with decorative wood brackets turns the dead zone along a soffit into an attention-grabber. Painted white against a pale blue wall, it's an ideal display space for colorful collections. Make your own with a piece of plywood and brackets cut to fit; find both at home-supply stores.

2 MADE-TO-ORDER CABINETRY. Wood lattice gives stock stile-and-rail doors a designer touch. Build your own by removing the solid center panels and replacing them with checkerboard-pattern grilles, available through renovator's-supply catalogs.

3 DECORATIVE MOLDINGS. A beadboard back and custom face frame accented with turned posts add instant architecture to an ordinary open base cabinet. Put together your own frame using stock porch parts you can find through a renovator's-supply catalog.

A hanging plate rack doubles as a dramatic window treatment.

← GO FOR AN UPDATED FARMHOUSE FEEL

4 PENDANTS WITH PATINA. Repro lights can cost more than the real deals. You pay for new wiring and the ease of not having to wade through salvage yards. But these days many dealers refurbish their old lights—and besides, the search is half the fun.

5 METAL BACKSPLASH. A nod to commercial kitchen backsplashes, inexpensive galvanized-steel roofing forms a fire-safe barrier between the range and the wall.

6 ZINC-TOPPED PREP TABLE. Use a potting bench to stand in for an island; its shelf can hold pots for cooking just as easily as ones for planting. Finish it to match your cabinets, or use an accent color to make it a focal point.

7 SKIRTED SINK. A curtain on a rod bought for a few bucks hides cleaning supplies and plumbing and adds a welcome hit of color. Buy a fabric remnant for a little bit more, then stitch it yourself or have a tailor sew it to your specs.

→ TRY THE LIVED-IN LOOK

8 PRETTY PENDANTS. Dress up your task lighting. Convert a recessed can with a pendant-light adapter and fabric shade, for about $20 through home catalogs.

9 REPURPOSED POT RACK. For a DIY version of this custom wrought-iron rack, mount a section of salvaged iron fencing so the rails run horizontally, and hang pots from hooks on the rails.

10 RECLAIMED ISLAND. A country store "seed and bean" counter offers twice the charm for half the price of a carpenter-built island. Search salvage yards and flea markets for rustic, unrestored versions like this one.

→ GIVE IT RUSTIC CHARM

11 FREESTANDING HUTCH. A piece of furniture offers all the storage of a custom built-in for a fraction of the cost. Expect to pay about $700 for a vintage wood step-back cupboard like this one at antiques stores, or less at a tag or estate sale.

12 PATTERNED WALLS. White-painted metal ceiling tiles used as wall cladding add new dimension to the room. Install them floor-to-ceiling, or only halfway up as a wainscot capped with a wood chair rail. Save on paint by using tiles finished with a white satin-powder coat. Expect to pay about $13 per 2-square-foot tile from a vintage-supply catalog.

← ADD HARDWORKING APPEAL

13 WALL RUNNER. Use expensive finishes sparingly. This single strip of blue subway tile behind the range makes an oceanic impact.

14 PRO-STYLE WINE STORAGE. Keep bottles in a vintage wood riddling rack like this one. Once used by French champagne producers to stow fermenting bubbly, the salvaged racks double as wine cellars. Find them through an online auction site.

15 STONE FLOOR. Bring outdoor materials indoors. Patio pavers are long-wearing, easy to clean, and inexpensive. For extra thrift, search remnants at flooring stores.

✳ TOH DESIGN ADVICE

When shopping for online deals, check websites frequently and sign up for daily alerts, since many promotions last for one day only.

← PROVIDE PERIOD DETAILS

16 LIGHT-DIFFUSING SHADES. Reduce glare with semi-sheer fabric shades. These relaxed romans are custom, but the same look can be found ready to install at big-box stores for about $20 apiece or less.

17 WHITEWASHED WALLS. Lighten the look of wood paneling by brushing on a white-tinted glaze. Here, the finish softens busy grain patterns in knotty pine.

18 DECORATIVE BRACKETS. Boost style with carved wood supports, such as these white-painted ones propping up open shelves and a breakfast bar. Find them starting at about $7 each at home-supply stores.

→ CRAFT A COUNTRY LOOK

19 TWO-TONE CABINETRY. Call out inset or partial overlay doors and drawer fronts by painting them a different shade from the cabinet boxes. Here, soft blue set against a white-sand background evokes a beachside retreat.

20 RUSTIC PANELING. Add texture to smooth drywall— as well as scuff protection in high-traffic areas, such as this kitchen and the hallway leading up to it—with a mixture of V-groove paneling and lap siding. Opt for thrifty versions like textured plywood, available at home-supply stores.

→ GET SOME RETRO COOL

21 OVERSIZE TASK LIGHTS.
Put pendants above the kitchen island. They're classier than track lighting or recessed cans, and can cost less too. The large-scale aluminum ones at right echo the shine of the faucet and cabinet hardware, tying the kitchen's details together.

22 COLORFUL CABINETRY.
Reinvent dark wood or white cabinets by painting them a refreshing hue. Here, a pale sage green reminiscent of Jadite dishware balances the intensity of the red floor.

23 VINTAGE-LOOK FLOOR.
Add some oomph with a new floor made of an old-school material: linoleum. It's easy to clean, naturally antimicrobial, and comes in more than a dozen shades, such as this vibrant red. Prices start at about $5 per square foot.

✳ TOH DESIGN ADVICE

If a friend or neighbor is also renovating, see what you can buy together since many items are cheaper—or more negotiable—when purchased in multiples.

→ BUDGET-SMART STORAGE SOLUTIONS

24 COUNTRY CUPBOARD DOORS. Replace solid center panels with chicken wire to showcase dishes. Buy a roll for cheap at a hardware store.

25 BAR-INSPIRED GLASS RACK. Use the underside of open shelves to store wine glasses and champagne flutes. Find stemware holders at home-supply stores.

26 PRO-CHEF UTENSIL BAR. Hang cooking essentials from S-hooks on a stainless rail. Look for these at restaurant- or home-supply stores.

27 CUSTOMIZED CONTAINERS. Vary the height of clutter-controlling baskets to correspond with their contents. A low-cost set of small, medium, and large baskets can be found online from home-furnishing stores.

28 CAFÉ-STYLE CUP HOLDERS. Hooks screwed into the bottom of open shelving dangle a vibrant array of mugs. Find them through online hardware stores.

29 WHITEWASHED WINE RACK. Stack and glue together 1-foot sections of painted terra-cotta drainpipe for a compact wine "cellar" in an open storage cubby. Get precut round pipes like the ones shown, as well as self-supporting hexagonal ones from building-supply stores.

SALVAGED-WOOD cabinets made from old oak floor joists and accented with walnut give this kitchen a time-honored feel. The stamped-metal ceiling is 100 years old, though it's as good as new, having been stored and never used.

CHAPTER 3 >
THE VINTAGE-LOOK KITCHEN

Whether your house is two years old or two centuries old, using traditional period details in your kitchen is a sure way to add warmth and get a look with longevity. Flat-panel cabinets, stone slab counters, stamped-metal ceilings, subway tiles, and factory lights have all stood the test of time. And, as the examples in the upcoming pages prove, their simple, utilitarian good looks and inherent durability allow them to blend equally well with today's hardworking stainless steel.

before +afters

A new stamped-metal ceiling fits the Victorian-era home. →

↑ A refurbished 1950s Chambers stove inspired the rest of the room.

COZY CLASSIC

PROBLEM> Few appliances and small metal cabinets left the sad kitchen sorely under-equipped.
SOLUTION> Remove a wall to reconfigure the work-space with a peninsula, then add period touches inspired by the focal point: a vintage range.

FEW ROOMS ARE MORE APPEALING than a bright, open kitchen that invites family and friends to gather round. So after this couple gutted the make-shift cooking space in their 1852 cottage, they wanted to connect the kitchen to an adjacent family room, using a peninsula with stool seating on one side to delineate the two. The open-plan configuration would also keep the focus on the crowd-pleasing 1950s Chambers range that inspired the room's period look.

The couple took on most of the work themselves, with plenty of help from the wife's woodworker dad, who salvaged the original heart-pine floor and built the Shaker-style cabinets. Sweat equity freed up funds in the couple's budget for updating the wiring, plumbing, and gas lines, as well as an overhaul of the old stove. With one wall down, two dreary spaces became one cheery family-room kitchen with a separate table for playing games and doing crafts with their young daughter. The new space, together with the mini mudroom they created in an entry alcove, honors the history of the home and functions much more efficiently, says the husband. Which is another way of saying they nailed the period look and got the family-friendly upgrade they needed, too.

after

With one wall gone in favor of a peninsula, flat-panel cabinets provide just enough storage. To keep the look open and airy, uppers were painted white and base units a pale blue-green.

AN L-SHAPED WORK AREA defines the kitchen while remaining open to the family room.

Open shelves keep the look bright and clean and put essentials within reach.
↓

the plan

AFTER

Clear food-prep and cooking zones are established within the space, now open to the family room.

BEFORE

The existing kitchen was walled off from the family room and had a makeshift layout with almost no counter space.

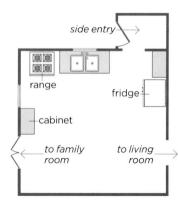

side entry →

range

fridge

cabinet

← to family room

to living room →

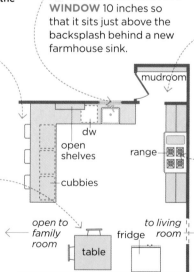

3 RAISED THE EXISTING WINDOW 10 inches so that it sits just above the backsplash behind a new farmhouse sink.

4 CREATED A MINI MUDROOM in the entry space, with a narrow bench, baskets, and coat hooks.

1 REMOVED THE WALL between the kitchen and family room and built a peninsula with cabinet storage.

2 ADDED A TABLE AND CHAIRS for a breakfast area that can double as an additional prep zone.

mudroom

dw

open shelves

cubbies

range

← open to family room

to living room →

fridge

table

5 RELOCATED THE STOVE to form a work triangle with the new sink and the old fridge, which was moved.

the details

↓**A REFURBISHED 1950S CHAMBERS STOVE** inspired the room's vintage style. The birch plywood cabinets and detailed vent-hood surround were built and painted by the wife's father. The countertops are Crema Marfil marble. The husband made the mudroom bench from salvaged wood.

↓**THE CHERRY CUTTING BOARD,** made by the husband, sits snugly on the edges of the traditional farmhouse sink.

↑**STAMPED-METAL CEILING TILES** were installed by the husband. The pendant lights are reproductions, so they all match.

←**OPEN SHELVES** were painted off-white to match the walls, while a pale blue-green grounds the base units.

SMART SAVE

If you aren't sure about cabinet pulls, invest in three samples and see what works. You might blow about $25, but it beats buyer's remorse.

The wide cascading arch leading to the dining room echoes another in the house.

before The old bare-bones kitchen led to a butler's pantry at one end and a hall outside the laundry at the other.

SPANISH REVIVAL

PROBLEM> A plain galley kitchen bore no relation to the architecture of the rest of the 1930 house. **SOLUTION>** Reintroduce style-appropriate details including archways, a tile mural, and hand-painted scrollwork.

EVEN THE MOST INTACT VINTAGE HOUSE rarely has a wonderful period kitchen. This couple put up with a shoddy galley in their otherwise distinctive 1930 Spanish Revival house for over a decade. Bad enough were the worn cabinets and awkward layout, but the room also lacked the details found throughout their home, which has arched doorways, wrought-iron work, and an art-tile fireplace surround. The wife, an avid cook, craved a top-notch range, and with three children the family needed more food storage.

The solution delivered both without adding on. By absorbing a small butler's pantry, the kitchen gained needed square footage, allowing for more counter space, a snack peninsula, two sinks, an alcove for the pro-style range, and a double refrigerator-freezer. But as much as they like their new conveniences, the couple also love the new old-style architectural details: two cascading archways, triple-arched casement windows, and painted scrollwork. Says the husband, "We finally have a kitchen that measures up to the rest of the house."

↑ Decorative paint accents mimic original designs on beams in the living room.

after Annexing the pantry allowed for a long run of countertop with two sinks and a breakfast bar, as well as a 60-inch refrigerator.

THE VINTAGE-LOOK KITCHEN
> SPANISH REVIVAL

→ **THE STOVE ALCOVE,** set off with a cascading arch and hand-painted-tile mural, highlights the showpiece range.

↓ **A SNACK BAR** doubles as a homework station for the three kids.

■ **AFTER**

The kitchen now opens up to the dining room via a wide arch and has a long counter and small breakfast bar. The range alcove is in line with the fridge for a clean look.

the plan

BEFORE

The freestanding stove and refrigerator had little adjacent counter space; a butler's pantry added two extra doorways.

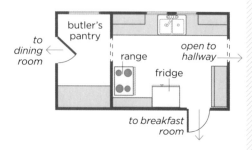

butler's pantry
to dining room
range
open to hallway
fridge
to breakfast room

1 ANNEXED THE BUTLER'S PANTRY that led to the dining room, removing one wall and creating a wide archway in the other. This made space for an extended counter and breakfast bar on one side and a 60-inch fridge on the other.

2 REPLACED THE WINDOWS with identical sets of triple-arched casement models that echo arches throughout the house.

3 ADDED ARCHES in two places. The doorway to the adjacent hall got a simple Roman curve; the alcove for the range got a cascading arch.

4 BUILT IN A HUTCH with a serving counter along the entry to the breakfast room.

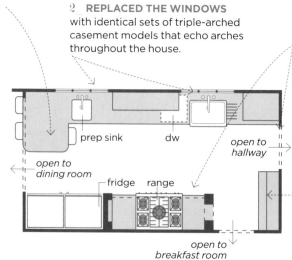

prep sink
dw
open to dining room
open to hallway
fridge
range
open to breakfast room

← A BUILT-IN HUTCH on the way to the breakfast room features a plate rack, mahogany serving counter, and cascading-arch detailing. Upper shelves keep a collection of cookbooks within easy reach.

EASY UPGRADE

Line an open cabinet or cupboard with beadboard or V-groove paneling to enhance its vintage appeal.

↓ NEW ARCHITECTURAL DETAILS, such as the curved brackets beneath the upper cabinets and the pull-open casement windows, reflect the Spanish Revival style of the 1930 house.

↑ GROOVES IN THE SOAPSTONE COUNTER create a drainboard; they're graded to encourage water to run into the basin.

TOH DESIGN ADVICE

Stay flexible. You might decide on a certain type of flooring, then pull up the existing one to find terrific wood original to the house.

← THE FARMHOUSE SINK is a period-appropriate choice, and its deep basin conceals dirty dishes.

EASY UPGRADE

Switch out a wood windowsill for one made of stone or solid surfacing that matches the countertop. This turns it into a handsome water- and weather-resistant decorative accent.

The curved edge of the marble-topped island's seating area makes it convivial for casual dining.

TWIST ON TRADITIONAL

PROBLEM> **A busy family needed a cook space that could handle lots of action and always look good.**
SOLUTION> **Use two islands and made-to-measure cabinets to make this on-display kitchen look perfectly polished.**

IT MAY BE THE ULTIMATE DREAM KITCHEN, but what makes it work is its down-to-earth approach: There's a place for everything—and everyone—in this home's friendly, high-functioning command center. The comfortable, almost country feel of the space reflects the classic architectural style of the house as well as the lifestyle of its owners.

Custom maple cabinets have the look of old-time cupboards with turned legs, flat-panel doors, and painted and glazed finishes. While the kitchen is fairly compact and easy to navigate, its 10-foot-high ceilings give the impression of grandeur. It also allows for stacking cabinets right up to the wide crown molding with a stretch of narrow divided-light flip-up doors across the top. Appliances suit the owners' penchant for entertaining at home, providing them with a 60-inch pro-style range, twin 36-inch refrigerators camouflaged behind custom panels, four freezer drawers, and a wine cooler—as well as a microwave, a warming drawer, and a built-in coffee station. The result is a kitchen with a timeless look and the kind of long-lasting, high-quality materials that will serve it for years to come.

A cookbook niche in the island becomes a decorative accent with an arched cutout. →

↓ **A SECOND ISLAND,** topped with maple, bracketed with columns, and fitted with open shelves and cabinets, separates the kitchen from the family room. Eliminating a wall here also allows the windowless kitchen to channel natural light from the adjoining space.

↑ **THE MARBLE-TOPPED ISLAND** with bar seating puts family and friends in proximity to the cook, who is just steps away from sink, stove, and storage aplenty.

the plan

BEFORE + AFTER

A pair of islands provides plenty of counter space and keeps cooking and socializing together yet separate, to eliminate traffic jams. Floor-to-ceiling cabinets help corral clutter in a kitchen that's wide open to the family room.

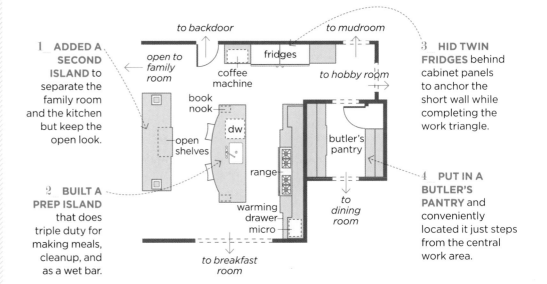

1 **ADDED A SECOND ISLAND** to separate the family room and the kitchen but keep the open look.

2 **BUILT A PREP ISLAND** that does triple duty for making meals, cleanup, and as a wet bar.

3 **HID TWIN FRIDGES** behind cabinet panels to anchor the short wall while completing the work triangle.

4 **PUT IN A BUTLER'S PANTRY** and conveniently located it just steps from the central work area.

to backdoor

open to family room

fridges

coffee machine

to mudroom

to hobby room

book nook

dw

open shelves

butler's pantry

range

to dining room

warming drawer
micro

to breakfast room

the details

↓ A HIDDEN WARMING DRAWER keeps food at the right temperature till it's time to serve—a big help when hosting a dinner party.

← THE LIGHTING includes low-voltage pucks to illuminate cabinet interiors and undersides.

SMART SAVE

Hang glass-front doors from stock cabinets on their sides to get a custom effect for narrow top units.

↓ A GLASS-FRONT SPICE CABINET puts a sampling of glass jars on display while helping the rest stay neatly organized and close at hand.

↑ THE BUILT-IN ESPRESSO AND COFFEE MACHINE unclutters the counter. The unit can share a water line with the fridge.

The existing stamped-metal ceiling tiles required only a fresh coat of paint.

The original (nonworking) coal stove provides an atmospheric focal point.

after

New Shaker-style cabinets have a time-honored look. The old brick hearth was painted white to set off the 125-year-old iron coal stove. The deep-green granite island countertop visually balances the dark stove.

VICTORIAN UPDATE

PROBLEM> The kitchen had survived many years and owners, at the expense of its charm and function.
SOLUTION> Do a historically sympathetic remodel that quietly incorporates modern conveniences and more expansive workspaces.

KITCHEN REMODELS ARE COMPLICATED BEASTS anywhere, but even more so in a historic house, where modern efficiency often seems at odds with charming detail. Such was the quandary facing the owner of this 1883 home, which, despite a bumpy history as a girls' school and a boardinghouse, was in near-original condition. Unfortunately the kitchen was dysfunctional, with storage and cleanup space shunted into a pantry and no running water (the previous owners took the freestanding sink with them). An adjacent breakfast room was accessible only through another pantry, with a second kitchen (including a sink) grafted on awkwardly at one end.

Despite these flaws, the homeowner did not want a spanking new space. "I'd seen too many old houses with fabulous kitchens that looked totally out of place," he says. "I wanted the same old kitchen, but much nicer." Ultimately, his architect and contractor gave him just that—with one big change. The kitchen now flows directly into the breakfast room, which retains a cleanup sink but gave most of its plumbed area over to a new half bath. The stamped-metal ceiling, original iron stove, and pine floors remain. In fact, without a close look, you might not know that a major renovation took place here. Exactly how the owner wanted it.

Door panels and a custom cabinet help the fridge blend into its surroundings. ↓

Curvy brackets add a graceful, old-fashioned detail beneath the island counter. ←

↑ **THE WORKTABLE** next to the corner stove provides the necessary landing space. Its open lower shelf keeps oversize pots and pans where they're needed.

AFTER
The original kitchen has new cabinets, appliances, and prep space, and now connects to the breakfast room, which still has its own sink.

the plan

BEFORE
The one-time boardinghouse's kitchen was closed off from a breakfast room with a kitchen of its own.

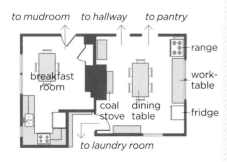

to mudroom   to hallway   to pantry

breakfast room

coal stove   dining table

range

work-table

fridge

to laundry room

1 **CUT AN OPENING** between the kitchen and breakfast room to improve traffic flow while preserving the original kitchen's footprint.

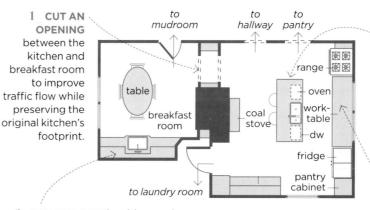

to mudroom   to hallway   to pantry

table

breakfast room

coal stove

range

oven

work-table

dw

fridge

pantry cabinet

to laundry room

2 **WALLED OFF** the old second kitchen (putting that space to use as a powder room) and built a new cabinet wall with sink.

3 **BUILT AN ISLAND** with a double sink, dishwasher, and second oven for improved work flow, more prep space, and snack seating.

4 **PUT IN A NEW WORKTABLE** that evokes vintage kitchens while accommodating the existing windows.

the details

→ **OPEN SHELVES,** glass-front cabinets, and a Delft-tile backsplash lighten up the breakfast room's cabinet wall.

↓ **HANDY STORAGE** for spices and other small items hides behind doors in the nonworking coal stove.

↑ **A BRACKETED SHELF** running along the top of the old stove wall displays heirloom transferware plates.

↑ **SLIDE-OUT SHELVES** provide easy access to dry goods in a tall, deep pantry cupboard.

← **THE ANTIQUE STOVE** and its hearth make the past present in the remodeled kitchen. A new passageway to the breakfast room is lined with books and display pieces.

The kitchen had a nice oak floor but an awkwardly shaped island, a poorly placed fridge, and bland finishes.

before

FORMAL GEORGIAN

PROBLEM> The basic layout worked, but an odd island and dated finishes didn't.
SOLUTION> Leave the floor plan as is but move the fridge and replace everything else for a dressed-up, new-old look.

ASK FOUR STRONG-MINDED PEOPLE to collaborate on a kitchen design and you may get open warfare. But call on product and graphic designers who also happen to be the homeowners, a kitchen designer, and a carpenter-contractor, and you'll get a high-functioning, sophisticated setting for cooking and socializing alike—in less than three months. The husband and wife assembled their dream team after four years of bumping into each other amid the pickled-oak cabinets and fluorescent lights of their Georgian-style house's 1980s kitchen. The husband, who refurbishes antique clocks and light fixtures as a hobby, craved a coffered ceiling that would show off a prized chandelier; the wife wanted an island packed with drawers and topped with pale marble.

The contractor saw ways to widen a passageway and case it in 18th-century style, and the kitchen designer worked her magic with off-the-shelf cabinets and accessories, assembling them to create custom-look pieces like the island and a ceiling-height hutch full of old-fashioned character. Today, the kitchen's a pleasure to work in: Everything is right where it's supposed to be, and the couple no longer bump into each other. Says the wife, "Friends, kids, grandkids—everyone gravitates to the kitchen and just enjoys it."

↑
The hutch was created from two cabinets, a cherry-stained counter, and footed base trim.

after

Vintage-green cabinets, new appliances, stone counters, and a better layout create a sense of spaciousness within the same footprint.

Get the vintage look

TIPS FROM
COLETTE SCANLON,
TOH DESIGN EDITOR

1 Use at least three finishes.
Combine painted with both natural and stained cabinetry for a kitchen that looks like it was added onto over time.

2 Add furniture details.
Footed base trim on cabinets and turned legs on islands make even stock cabinets look like heirlooms.

3 Mix up the countertops.
Use both wood and stone surfaces to reinforce a furnished look.

4 Expose some shelves.
Display dishware and collectibles to give the kitchen a feeling of history.

5 Go for unique touches.
Try combining cabinet handles and knobs in different styles and materials to get an eclectic effect.

Display shelves show favorite pieces and contribute to the kitchen's airy look. →

A TRIPLE WINDOW and deep sill bounce light off the limestone counter. The paneled dishwasher sits between sink and hutch.

the plan

BEFORE
With its swinging door, single small window, and bulky closet, the space felt needlessly cramped.

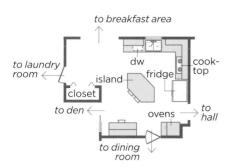

AFTER
Lots of display shelves and two structural changes—a larger window unit over the sink and a wider opening to the dining room—made the space, still the same size, feel sunnier and roomier.

1 TURNED THE CLOSET into a niche for the microwave and refrigerator. Fridge drawers next to the cooktop keep butter and eggs close at hand.

2 BUILT A NEW ISLAND that fits the classic style of the house. Drawers facing the cleanup and dining areas mean no more hunting for platters and napkins.

3 SWAPPED OUT THE SINK WINDOW for a triple unit set flush with the facade to create a deep, light-inviting sill.

4 HID A PIPE CHASE behind false cabinet doors to give the oven wall a seamless look.

5 REPLACED A SWINGING DOOR with a more centered passageway lined with backlit display cabinets.

the details

→ **INEXPENSIVE STEEL RAILS** hold pot lids at the ready.

EASY UPGRADE

If you're running stone countertops up the wall as a backsplash, have the fabricator add a small shelf along the top. It will give the wall a more finished look and provide you with bonus display space.

↑ **CUSTOM GLASS-FRONT CABINETS** in white line the passageway between the kitchen and the dining room. On the adjacent wall, stock cabinets were stacked to create a pantry, with filler strips closing any gaps.

← **THE COFFERED CEILING,** painstakingly mapped and remapped to fit around lights and cabinetry, reflects the home's traditional architecture.

← **CHERRY-STAINED POSTS** made by the cabinet company and bronze knobs found at a home center helped turn an assembly of stock cabinets into a furniture-like island, with drawers on three sides.

The cherry island, with its turned legs, evokes a vintage kitchen table. →

The kitchen's metal cabinets left it feeling sterile and out of sync.

CRAFTSMAN STYLE

PROBLEM> The 1980s kitchen didn't fit the style of the 1908 house.
SOLUTION> Add cherry cabinets, reproduction lighting, and other Arts and Crafts details.

IT CAN BE A CHALLENGE to find an old home's true personality under the onion-like layers of improvements. When the owners of a 1908 Craftsman house decided to rework a poorly laid-out addition that held a cold 1980s kitchen, they had to find a way to channel the space's long-obliterated Arts and Crafts spirit. One thing was clear: Nothing about the walled-off kitchen worked—neither its utilitarian style and lack of seating nor its isolation from other rooms.

After two years of scribbling ideas on napkins, the couple called in an architect to help them integrate the kitchen, which was isolated in its separate wing, and make it feel like it was always part of the house. Because the whole wing needed a more livable layout, the solution was to relocate the kitchen to where the breakfast room had been, bump out for an eating nook and pantry, and put a new family room in the old kitchen's space. The remodel established an easy flow from the kitchen to the adjoining dining room in the main part of the house and among the spaces in the reconfigured wing. The new kitchen's warm cherry cabinets, paneled range hood, and crown molding, as well as reproduction Craftsman-inspired light fixtures, fit the old house's period style to a T. Still, its granite counters and muscular appliances are very much of the moment. Says the wife, "What people notice most is that, though the kitchen looks new, it fits in so well with the rest of the house."

Cherry cabinets, granite counters, and a copper-flecked backsplash add warmth. Island-side seating means the cook's never alone.

The light fixture echoes one that hangs over the dining-room table.

→ **A BAY-WINDOW BUMPOUT** opened up the kitchen, offering views from clear across the room and well into the backyard.

AFTER

The kitchen moved to the breakfast room space and gained a breakfast nook, which leads to a new butler's pantry and side entry. The stairs were moved to a new family room built where the old kitchen had stood.

the plan

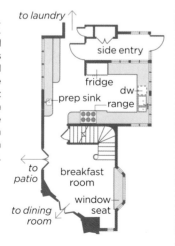

BEFORE
The U-shaped kitchen was separated from the breakfast room by a staircase. The dining room was even farther away.

to laundry
side entry
fridge
dw
prep sink
range
to patio
breakfast room
window seat
to dining room

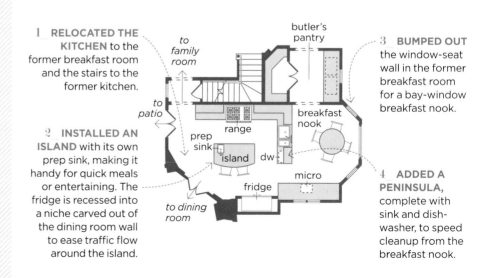

1 **RELOCATED THE KITCHEN** to the former breakfast room and the stairs to the former kitchen.

2 **INSTALLED AN ISLAND** with its own prep sink, making it handy for quick meals or entertaining. The fridge is recessed into a niche carved out of the dining room wall to ease traffic flow around the island.

3 **BUMPED OUT** the window-seat wall in the former breakfast room for a bay-window breakfast nook.

4 **ADDED A PENINSULA,** complete with sink and dishwasher, to speed cleanup from the breakfast nook.

to family room
butler's pantry
to patio
prep sink
range
island
dw
breakfast nook
micro
fridge
to dining room

the details

→ **A CHERRY MANTEL** and paneling hide the vent hood. Earthy-brown granite covers every countertop in the kitchen.

→ **CHERRY CROWN MOLDING** was stained to match the trim in the dining and living rooms. The ceiling-hung cabinets over the peninsula have glass doors on all sides to bring light from the breakfast area to the kitchen.

The mosaic-tile backsplash reinforces the earth-tone Craftsman palette. ←

↑ **AN UNDER-COUNTER MICROWAVE** keeps a section of counter along the fridge wall clear of clutter. Located on the way to the breakfast nook, the counter serves as a staging area.

← **TURNED-LEG DETAILS** and paneled sides that match the rest of the custom cabinets give the center island the feel of freestanding furniture. The sink and granite top make it a hardworking prep area.

EASY UPGRADE

For a subtle contrast, hone an island's stone surface for a softer finish, and polish stone countertops (which take more of a beating) for a harder surface that needs less-frequent sealing.

Leaded-glass cabinet fronts reinforce the style of the 1920s house.

before The kitchen was tiny, utilitarian, and missing the fridge, which was around the corner in the pantry.

after

The range remains in its original location. Its vent hood is hidden by a painted wood valance topped with crown molding to resemble a mantel.

HIDE THE APPLIANCES

PROBLEM> While the kitchen was as old as the house, it lacked the same visual appeal. SOLUTION> Layer on period-appropriate details and conceal the stainless steel.

REDOING A KITCHEN IN A WELL-PRESERVED 1920s HOUSE requires equal regard for the past and the present, and that was clearly the case here. The homeowners longed for a high-performance cooking space with the latest built-in appliances but also craved a strong period style. Maintaining the character of the vintage house was paramount.

The couple kicked off the process by asking their designer to make the centerpiece of the kitchen an old-fashioned cast-iron range in fire-engine red, while hiding the other appliances and tweaking the layout only slightly. "We could have taken out a wall or put in an island," says the wife, "but we didn't want to forgo the flavor of the house." Not that function wasn't key too. Back-to-back sinks—mounted in a custom cherry hutch—offer prep and cleanup convenience, and a double-wide stack of stainless-steel appliances is tucked inside the pantry. To satisfy the desire for order, two symmetrical banks of to-the-ceiling cabinets are crowned, glazed, footed, and aligned right down to the height of the drawers. And the refrigerators? They blend into the cabinetry, hidden behind paneled doors on either side of the built-in china cabinet.

Metal grilles on top of column fridges let the compressors breathe. ↓

↑ **TWIN FRIDGES,** hidden behind matching door panels, create a unified look with the china cabinet.

the plan

BEFORE

The pantry held the fridge but was nearly walled off from the kitchen.

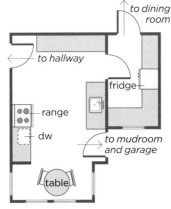

to dining room

to hallway

fridge

range

dw

to mudroom and garage

table

AFTER

The footprint remained the same but the fridge was relocated, with a twin, to the wall between the sink and the range, for a proper work triangle. The dishwasher moved into the pantry.

1 ELIMINATED A DOOR and moved the entry 18 inches to align it with the pantry opening.

2 BUILT IN A BREAKFAST NOOK sheltered by a curved ceiling and framed by an archway.

3 OPENED UP THE PANTRY by replacing a door with an arched opening.

4 GROUPED APPLIANCES in the pantry, including a dishwasher, steam oven, coffee station, wine fridge, and twin microwaves.

5 CUT OUT A PASS-THROUGH and surrounded it with a hutch that holds back-to-back sinks, one for food prep and one for cleanup.

to dining room

fridge   fridge

to hallway

built-in appliances

prep sink   clean-up sink

range

breakfast nook

to mudroom and garage

the details

→ **AN ARCHWAY** and a pass-through framed by a cherry hutch now connect the cooking area to the pantry, which holds a bank of stainless-steel built-in appliances.

↑ **BACK-TO-BACK SINKS,** with black granite counters, are framed by an opening in the hutch and share one swiveling single-handle faucet.

→ **THE BREAKFAST NOOK** has built-in banquettes and an arched ceiling. The table is made from a cast-iron base and a wood top painted to match the cabinets.

↑ **CRACKLE-GLAZED TILE** and a framed inset create a textured backsplash that doesn't upstage the range.

SMART SAVE

Use inexpensive field tile for a backsplash and save the more expensive stuff for an inset that serves as a focal point.

A CONTAINED WORK ZONE allows cooks to turn easily between prep areas. An island invites hosts and guests to socialize minus traffic jams.

CHAPTER 4

THE HOST KITCHEN

Whatever the occasion, the kitchen is inevitably where everyone ends up. So you want to make it hospitable for chef and guests alike. First, consider flow: Whether the space is large or small, keep the floor plan open when plotting areas for cooking, tasting, and conversation, so everybody can happily coexist. Be sure to provide plenty of places to gather, including an island or a peninsula and a big table or a cozy dining nook. Then add, if you can, an extra sink or fridge so guests can help—or just help themselves.

before +afters

1_ **Double the Size**

2_ **Twin Work Zones**

3_ **Open-Plan Great Room**

Murano-glass shades echo the room's color scheme and punch it up, too.

before In the old space, the worn-out fridge was awkwardly stuck in a corner near a now-relocated back door.

DOUBLE THE SIZE

PROBLEM> A narrow kitchen with its far-flung appliances couldn't handle an extended family. **SOLUTION>** Expand the footprint on two sides for twice as much square footage—and hospitality.

THERE'S TRUTH TO THE OLD SAW that you should live in a house for at least a year before embarking on a major renovation. For the owners of this 1930s house, make that seven. That's how long it took them to tackle the fake-wood cabinets, laminate counters, and vinyl flooring that came with the place. The delay was especially long considering that the husband's family business sells high-end kitchen cabinets. "People would come to the house expecting a gorgeous kitchen," he says. "Their jaws would drop in shock."

After a major renovation, the kitchen that emerged doubled the room's square footage and brightened the space with a palette of green and yellow. By bumping out the range wall and taking over a bedroom space, they expanded the footprint to include a large island that connects to a family table. Now there's plenty of room for dinner with their two daughters, 12 and 15, as well as extended family who frequently stop by—both husband and wife come from big Italian families where "everyone has to participate in meal preparation," says the wife. Long expanses of countertop accommodate many hands joining in the prep work; there are even his and hers sinks. "It's open, it's friendly, and we can have 22 people in the kitchen without feeling crowded," she says. "I'll never figure out what took us so long."

after Green upper cabinets are set off by yellow base cabinets topped with honed black granite. A built-in teak table forms a T with the center island to fit family and friends who like to pitch in.

Windows wrap both corners of the sink wall to maximize natural light. ↓

→ **THE BLACK GRANITE COUNTERS** provide a roomy landing area on either side of the range as well as continuous expanses of workspace for extended family to share in meal prep. The dark surfaces, along with the teak tabletop, lend an edge of sophistication to the otherwise pale color palette.

EASY UPGRADE

Consider giving an island a unique identity by wrapping it in a compatible paneling style. Beadboard complements flat- or raised-panel cabinet doors without matching them exactly.

the plan

BEFORE

The very basic kitchen felt cramped and outdated.

AFTER

Now twice as big after bumping out the range wall and taking over a bedroom, the remodeled space arranges the range, sink, and refrigerator in a U-shape layout.

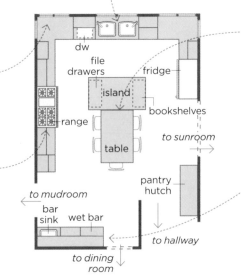

1 MAXIMIZED NATURAL LIGHT by minimizing upper cabinets along the sink wall to allow for lots of windows, including units that wrap the two corners.

2 BORROWED AND ADDED SPACE by bumping out the range wall and annexing footage from a bedroom and the dining room, which were both relocated.

3 INCLUDED SIDE-BY-SIDE SINKS, since he's a lefty and she's a righty. One sink has the faucet at the far left corner, the other at the right, so the couple can cook and clean up together.

4 CREATED AN ISLAND with a family table as an extension. Fearing a kitchen desk would always look messy, the homeowners opted instead for two file drawers in the island for household papers.

5 ADDED A WET BAR outside the dining room entry so that guests can help themselves.

↓ CURVED BRACKETS on the sides of the upper cabinets, built-in display shelves, and a beadboard backsplash add character to glass-front units.

← A CUSTOM-BUILT HUTCH with frosted-glass doors is the main food pantry in the kitchen. It was painted on-site, given a base coat of the same yellow as the cabinets, then topped with an antiqued finish to give it more of a furniture look.

↓ SCROLL-STYLE PEWTER PULLS and a beaded detail add decorative interest to the pantry drawers, which hold snacks for the kids.

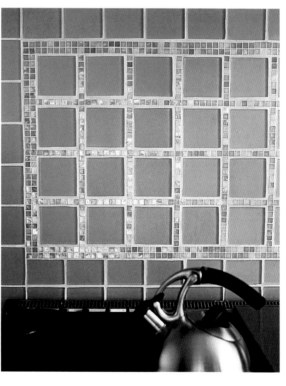

← HIGH-GLOSS GLASS MOSAIC TILES create a basketweave effect inset amid sanded-glass squares on the backsplash above the range.

← TURNED LEGS that mimic those supporting the teak table—but on a smaller scale—are set into a wood frame, adding an architectural accent to yellow sink cabinets.

The bare-bones space narrowed at one end with a doorway to the laundry area. *before*

TWIN WORK ZONES

PROBLEM> Frequent hosts needed room to prepare dinner parties for up to 20, and their apartment wasn't up to snuff.
SOLUTION> Annex adjacent nooks to add a second prep-and-cleanup area.

BUYING INTO A FORMER RENTAL can mean inheriting some slipshod spaces. While the footprint of this kitchen may have been original to the 1928 apartment, the contents—including the electric stove and vinyl floor—were left over from a recent, none-too-lavish remodel. The couple renting it loved to cook and had put up with the cheap redo before the unit was up for sale. Three years later, after buying it, they set about remaking the kitchen with enough room and storage to handle prepping for dinner parties.

The couple found room to expand by taking down a wall that divided the space from an adjacent breakfast nook at one end and removing a sliver of wall with a doorway to the laundry area at the other. Now one continuous galley, the enlarged kitchen has a peninsula with two stools where friends can hang out while the hosts are at the stove. There are two distinct prep-and-cleanup zones: one along the original sink wall and another in a butler's pantry alcove (where the washer and dryer had stood), complete with double ovens and the all-important second sink. "Having another sink helps when we're getting a meal and the table ready for guests," says the husband. "It also speeds cleanup." Soft-green granite covers five times more counter space than the kitchen had before, and a mix of flat-panel and beadboard-front cabinets—including a built-in hutch—triples the storage. Newly milled baseboard rings new oak flooring, both made to match originals in the rest of the rooms. The result: a hospitable new kitchen that blends beautifully with its period surroundings.

after

A granite-topped peninsula, next to the built-in china cabinet, provides a staging area for parties or a gathering spot that keeps guests and hosts in close proximity.

An adjustable-cord pulley light is a new interpretation of an early-20th-century shop task lamp. →

Glass-front upper cabinets frame a pretty display of dinnerware and glasses. →

Over the sink, crank-out casements are easier to open than double-hung windows. ↓

A LONG RUN of counter space along the range and sink wall allows prep, cooking, and cleanup to go on simultaneously.

the plan

AFTER
By removing walls and annexing adjacent spaces, the new design more than doubled the kitchen's square footage and made it a long galley.

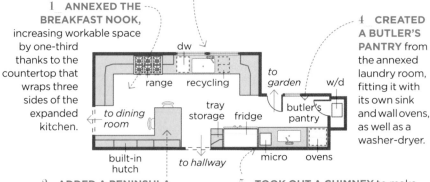

BEFORE
The original kitchen was walled off from both the breakfast nook and the laundry area.

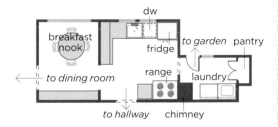

1 ANNEXED THE BREAKFAST NOOK, increasing workable space by one-third thanks to the countertop that wraps three sides of the expanded kitchen.

2 ADDED A PENINSULA opposite the range to provide an extra prep space as well as a spot for casual dining.

3 REVISED THE WINDOWS to make up for the loss of a large window in the former eating area. The sink window was enlarged by a foot along the sides, and at the top with the addition of a fanlight.

4 CREATED A BUTLER'S PANTRY from the annexed laundry room, fitting it with its own sink and wall ovens, as well as a washer-dryer.

5 TOOK OUT A CHIMNEY to make way for a second prep-and-cleanup zone that connects seamlessly with the main workspace.

the details

↓ BEADBOARD on the cabinets—mixed in with flat-panel door and drawer fronts—gives the cabinetry old-fashioned charm.

← A GANG OF APPLIANCES, including the refrigerator and double wall ovens, flanks the sink in the butler's pantry alcove, which serves as a second prep-and-cleanup zone.

↓ NEW ARCHED DOORWAYS in the kitchen looked so authentic that the couple added more in the apartment's other rooms. The curves are repeated in the fanlight over the sink, the edge of the exhaust hood, and in tiled niches flanking the cooktop.

↑ WHITE SUBWAY TILE covers the backsplash. It's interspersed with green-and-pink flower tiles, which the wife chose to suit the traditional style of the home and her husband's love of gardening.

← GRANITE COUNTERTOPS are veined like marble—the period-appropriate choice—but are far more stain resistant. Arched tile niches flanking the cooktop hold accent pieces and cooking oils.

before

OPEN-PLAN GREAT ROOM

PROBLEM> A dark and dreary kitchen demanded an attractive update in a short space of time.
SOLUTION> Leave the footprint alone but take down a wall to annex the family room, and swap a hemmed-in peninsula for a party-friendly island.

NOTHING MOVES A PROJECT FORWARD LIKE A DEADLINE. In this case, it was a daughter's announcement that she wanted to have her wedding reception at home—in just four months. The 1950s kitchen in her parents' ranch house was a decent size but not fit for company, with its outdated finishes and confined layout. A partial wall and a peninsula separated the kitchen from the family room, boxing in the cook. And though the couple had lived for 20 years with this less-than-perfect union of the two rooms, when their daughter shared her wedding wish they seized the opportunity to make some changes—fast.

The kitchen designer they turned to for help convinced them they had to keep the footprint if there was any chance of getting it done on time. They decided to open up the room by removing the peninsula and adding a big bay window. Clever built-ins and plenty of white paint made it feel even more spacious, as did an island facing the family room, "so the cook is kept in the loop during gatherings," says the designer. "Weddings included." And the wedding? It went off like the redo: without a hitch.

after

A bay window, white cabinets and backsplash, and an island add a feeling of roominess within the original footprint.

A ceiling-mount hood vents through the roof of the one-story house.

Cherry floors echo the island cabinets and stained ceiling beams.

THE HOST KITCHEN
> OPEN-PLAN GREAT ROOM

→ **SMART USE OF BUILT-INS** created distinct areas for cooking, dining, bill paying, and sitting around the fireplace.

↓ **THE GRANITE-TOPPED ISLAND** was angled to ease traffic flow while maximizing counter space.

The built-in hutch in the dining area backs up to kitchen cabinets. ↓

the plan

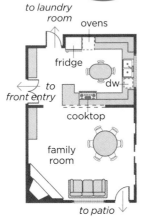

BEFORE
A peninsula boxed in the kitchen and separated it from the family room.

to laundry room
ovens
fridge
dw
to front entry
cooktop
family room
to patio ↓

AFTER
The peninsula came down in favor of an island, joining the two rooms into one.

1 **ADDED AN ISLAND** with seating, storage cabinets, and a sight line from cooktop to family room so that the cook can be part of the action.

2 **CREATED A DESK,** with its own storage, for the family room. The angled side allows for extra fireside seating.

3 **PUT IN A BAY WINDOW** to capture more natural light.

4 **STACKED CABINETS,** including an appliance garage, on what remained of the dividing wall, maximizing storage and prep space.

5 **BUILT A HUTCH** on the dining-area side of the dividing wall. A low cabinet caps the wall's exposed end.

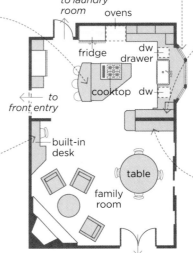

to laundry room
ovens
fridge
dw drawer
to front entry
cooktop
dw
built-in desk
table
family room
to patio ↓

the details

→ **THE RAISED SNACK BAR** on the cherry island helps hide the cooktop. At the end of the sink wall, what remains of the wall that separated kitchen and family room is filled with cabinets (the built-in hutch sits on its other side).

→ **A CHERRY COUNTERTOP** and antiqued-brass oak-leaf and bar pulls give the built-in hutch a distinctive, custom look. The recessed area provides another serving surface.

↑ **A PAINTED MANTEL SHELF** ties in with the white kitchen cabinets and updates the family room's 1950s brick fireplace.

← **DISPLAY SHELVES** are angled toward the seating area by the hearth. The desk area's bottom cabinet is designed to hold a speaker for a plasma TV.

SMART SAVE

Add a decorative accent and lighten the look of kitchen cabinets by leaving off a few doors. Unify the interior with a fresh coat of paint and fill with items you have on hand.

CHAPTER 5>
THE COLORFUL KITCHEN

Color can accomplish a lot. It can create a mood, highlight a room's best features (or camouflage its flaws), brighten a dark space, or expand a small one. Paint is the easiest, quickest, and most affordable way to add color, of course. But backsplash tile, countertops, and even appliances can inject a welcome pop, as well. Start with the hues you love, and you can't go wrong. Take a look at the ideas on the following pages to help inspire the rest of the transformation.

before +afters

before

Earlier upgrades brought in open shelves, white walls, and, later, bamboo floors and a niche for the fridge.

PAINT ADDS PIZZAZZ

PROBLEM> The white-on-white environment was devoid of personality.
SOLUTION> Plan a dramatic palette and roll on a few cans of paint to create a warm, cheerful space.

NOTHING REVIVES AN OLD ROOM like an energetic new color scheme. In this 1940s ranch house, a previous remodel left a washed-out white kitchen, save for the sensational 1945 stove the wife inherited from her mother. White beadboard and glass-front cabinets mixed with open shelves; a red vent hood and pendants helped tie in the vintage range. Still, the room looked a little tired.

So the couple called in a local colorist. She took one look at the light pouring in on three sides and drew up a palette befitting the sunny space, including bright yellow walls, a citron ceiling, and lime wainscoting. She set off the couple's colorful tableware, displayed in open shelves, with a dynamic turquoise backdrop that she also applied to the doors. Then she gave the room an edge, literally, with black trim around doors, windows, and floorboards. That revved-up range finally has surroundings that suit its playful spirit. Say the homeowners of the finished space, "It's fun and uplifting, and makes us smile."

after

The cabinets and counters stayed the same, but a carefully composed medley of colors makes the remodeled room as warm and welcoming as its 1940s stove.

↑
Yellow-green on the ceiling blends with the walls, making the small room feel bigger.

The tiniest details now pop: Painted light-switch covers keep the color rhythm going.

Pick the right palette

TIPS FROM
COLETTE SCANLON,
TOH DESIGN EDITOR

1 **Consider the effect and feeling you want.** If your goal is to make the room appear larger, go with lighter shades. But if you want to accentuate its coziness, opt for saturated hues. Also, warm colors draw in walls and other surfaces; cooler shades make them recede.

2 **Test colors on the wall.** Paint will be more intense than the color chip. If you're unsure, go a notch higher on the paint strip and select a paler version. Paint a swath at least 5 feet wide from floor to ceiling and apply two coats. Take a few days to live with the color and see how the light and furnishings in the room affect it; check out how it looks day and night. Painting on foamboard is another good option.

3 **Adopt the 60-30-10 rule.** To balance multiple colors, try using a dominant one for 60 percent of the room, a recessive one for 30 percent, and an accent color for 10 percent.

the plan

BEFORE + AFTER
The layout of the galley remains the same, with exterior doors at either end and an entryway to the living room.

↑**TURQUOISE PAINT**
on the back of the open black shelves visually balances the turquoise door framed by its black casing.

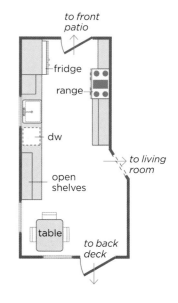

to front patio
fridge
range
dw
to living room
open shelves
table
to back deck

the details

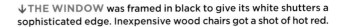

↓ **THE WINDOW** was framed in black to give its white shutters a sophisticated edge. Inexpensive wood chairs got a shot of hot red.

↓ **THE CEILING'S** yellow-green, a much warmer alternative to white, sets off the red-rimmed pendant lights.

↑ **OPEN SHELVES** gain new dimension with a graphic black frame and turquoise paint on the back.

↑ **GREEN WAINSCOTING** wraps the dining area while red accents, yellow walls, and a turquoise-and-black table tie it to the kitchen. The wood floor keeps it from going overboard.

← **THE 1945 RANGE** was a family heirloom; the new vintage-look range hood is a good match.

before

The old kitchen was closed off save for a narrow doorway and pass-through.

MID-CENTURY SCHEME

PROBLEM> The white kitchen was cramped, characterless, and walled off from the living room. SOLUTION> Take down a wall and introduce a two-tone color scheme that taps into the design origins of the 1950s ranch.

MOST RENOVATIONS START with plans on paper. This one started with a reciprocating saw. When the couple bought their 1950s ranch, they knew the kitchen would have to be completely overhauled. It had no counter space, old cabinets, and inefficient appliances. Since they wanted an open plan, the first order of business was to tear down the wall between the kitchen and living room. Still, the design stayed pretty sane: no pro-grade appliances, no glitzy surfaces, no carved-wood details.

The wife is a kitchen designer, and while she sees all the latest designs and products in the course of her job, she wanted features and finishes that suited the simplicity of the house. She chose concrete floors, engineered-stone counters, and contemporary bamboo base cabinets that mix with traditional flat-panel pantry doors and V-groove wall paneling for a kind of modern farmhouse look. Blocks of apple green and bright blue play off other colorful accents used throughout the house. The husband, a contractor, did much of the work, from gutting the room to the studs to running the electrical and staining the floors, which helped the couple stay within budget. Looking back on the four-month kitchen redo, the wife reflects, "We needed to change everything about the space functionally and aesthetically—and we did."

Apple-green upper cabinets paired with bamboo lowers give the room personality; bright hits of blue turn up the energy. The concrete slab foundation, exposed when vinyl flooring was removed, was cleaned and colored with an acid-based stain. Toekicks were built 1 inch higher than normal to allow for future installation of wood or tile.

Engineered stone resembles the real thing but is nonporous so it won't stain.

Green crown molding unifies upper cabinets spaced out along the walls. ↓

↑ **THE ISLAND** is large enough to comfortably accommodate meals but small enough that traffic can still flow around it to cook and cleanup stations.

AFTER

Removing the wall shared with the living room and closing up the back door made way for a handy U-shape design with counters, cabinetry, and appliances on the existing three walls.

the plan

BEFORE

The old kitchen had little counter space and a doorway interrupting the L-shape layout.

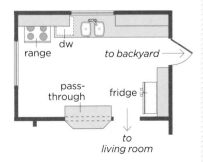

1 **INSTALLED A COOKTOP** under one of the two windows. A pop-up downdraft vent exhausts heat and odors.

2 **ADDED AN ISLAND** that offers seating for two, plus shelves and pull-out bins on the sink side.

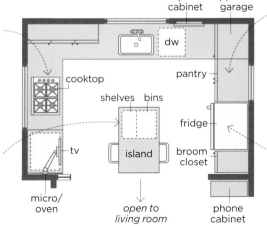

3 **CLOSED UP A BACK DOOR** for a U-shape layout. Food storage is contained in tall pantry cabinets. A small window was added up high.

4 **MOVED THE FRIDGE** to make room for a 15-inch-wide broom closet that hides away mops and brooms.

→ THE BAMBOO TELEPHONE CABINET around the living-room corner echoes the kitchen's base cabinets and creates a dedicated message center. The vivid blue wall contrasts with the kitchen's apple-green cabinets.

↓ THE MICROWAVE AND WALL OVEN are housed in a cabinet topped by a TV. The TV is mounted on an articulating bracket for viewing from anywhere in the kitchen.

← SMALL-APPLIANCE STORAGE is provided by cabinets that run right down to the countertop, keeping clutter to a minimum.

EASY UPGRADE

Protect chip-prone countertops by retrofitting appliance garages with roll-out shelves to ease pulling out heavy mixers and the like.

↑ THE CUSTOM SPICE CABINET is designed like a bathroom medicine chest, with a chalkboard where the mirror would be.

← THE FAUX APRON-FRONT SINK was made by facing the front of a 30-inch stainless-steel undermount sink with the same engineered stone used for the countertop and backsplash.

BLUE MAKES IT COOL

PROBLEM> **Rustic cabinets reinforced the claustrophobia of a kitchen crammed into a corner.** SOLUTION> **Annex an adjacent room to enlarge the footprint and keep the look airy with a pale blue-and-white color scheme.**

KNOCK YOURSELF OUT UPGRADING A WEEKEND GETAWAY, and don't be surprised if you start hanging your hat there seven nights a week. That's what happened to the couple who bought this 1880s foursquare as a beach retreat—only to realize that with a little TLC it might qualify as a year-round haven.

Previous owners had carved out a rental unit at the back of the house, with a knotty-pine kitchen and sadly sloped floor. The owners decided to reinstate the home's cook space there, knocking down a wall to annex a bath and opening up a staircase that had been blocked off. Traffic flow was smoothed by angling the counter near the back door. The traditional-style cabinets, crown molding, and mantelpiece over the range could have appeared quite staid but got a refreshing new look with cool blue paint and a warm brown glaze. Stainless-steel appliances, gray granite countertops, and a muted porcelain-tile floor give the space a clean and airy feel. "We thought we'd be out just on weekends," says one of the homeowners. "But now we've decided to move here full-time." The new kitchen, it seems, is quite a draw.

Blue cabinets and glossy white tile give the expanded space a real lift. Gray-veined granite plays off the stainless-steel appliances.

after

Reeded-glass top panels create the look of stacked cabinets at much less cost.

107

→ **THE PENINSULA,** a magnet during breakfast and cocktail hour, was made with a cabinet and coordinated posts, which tie the gathering spot to the cooking space.

↓ **CUSTOM CABINETS**
enclose the microwave and fridge for a neat, flush look.

the plan

BEFORE
The kitchen had room for a table but was low on prep and storage space.

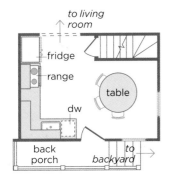

AFTER
Enlarged by one-third after annexing a bath, the kitchen gained prep and storage space. It's now a combination of cook's kitchen and social hub.

1 **ANNEXED A BATH** and closed up one window to create a solid cooking space with the range at its center.

2 **ANGLED A COUNTER AND CABINET** to improve flow around the peninsula.

3 **WIDENED THE PASSAGEWAY** to the dining room (formerly the living room) and added pocket doors.

4 **OPENED UP A BACK STAIRCASE** that had been boxed in to convert the house to two units.

5 **BUILT A BREAKFAST PENINSULA** with a cabinet, posts, and an inexpensive countertop.

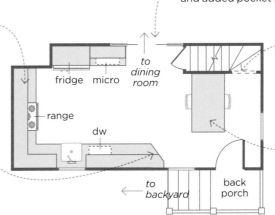

↓ REEDED-GLASS INSETS and interior lighting add interest to expanses of wood in the nearly ceiling-height cabinet fronts.

← UNEXPECTED SPLASHES OF COLOR give the staircase its own identity, while the peninsula's base connects it to the kitchen.

EASY UPGRADE
Recess a shallow cabinet—minus its door—for display shelves to perk up an empty expanse of wall.

↓ A PULLOUT on the range wall keeps spices and other provisions close at hand. The fluted column to its right helps give the range wall its fitted, finished look.

↑ AN EXTRA SLIVER OF CABINET SPACE makes the peninsula more functional. Cement-colored porcelain floor tile doesn't show dirt.

← GLOSSY SUBWAY TILES, painstakingly trimmed to create a herringbone pattern, play off a formal mantel with corbels that hides the range hood.

Multicolored tiles pull together the various hues of cabinets and walls. →

before The kitchen was short on counter space, drafty in winter, and bereft of charm.

VINTAGE NEUTRALS

PROBLEM> A century-old addition separated dining from a work area that had next to no prep space. **SOLUTION>** Blend salvaged wood, painted cabinetry, cement tile, and stainless steel to give the circa-1900-style kitchen a 21st-century edge.

SOMETIMES THE BEST WAY OUT OF A BAD KITCHEN is to salvage what you can and recycle the rest. In the case of this Victorian-era rowhouse, the kitchen's best features were limited to big windows and the breakfast room's built-in hutch. Grafted onto the house around 1900, the kitchen was completely cut off from the dining area, save for a door, and its ancient wiring and lack of counter space inspired odd daily routines—like setting the coffee grinder down on the radiator to plug it in to one of only two outlets. In winter, cold air whistled through one of the cabinets.

Working as a team, the homeowners tore out the cabinetry, sink, appliances, and dividing wall—selling what they could through online classifieds and taking the rest to a recycling center—then opened walls as needed for insulation, plumbing, and wiring. In went raised-panel cabinets with doors that echo the existing hutch. A mix of slate blue and grayish tan for island, hutch, and cabinets keeps the look unfitted and more appropriate to the era of the house. Black-walnut floors, soapstone counters, a table island topped with reclaimed fir, stainless-steel appliances, and LED lights make the space high-functioning yet cozy. A multicolored cement-tile backsplash ties together colors and materials used throughout the newly enlarged space. The result: period-appropriate charm and contemporary function.

after Bigger, prettier, and more comfortable too, the space's updated period look comes from an eclectic mix of colors and materials, including wood, stone, and tile.

The colorful, hard-wearing backsplash is made from cement floor tiles.

↑THE STAINLESS-STEEL RANGE HOOD seems to disappear into the backsplash pattern as it mimics the angularity of the medallions.

the plan

AFTER
Annexing the breakfast room created space for an island and countertops along two walls of the now-spacious galley.

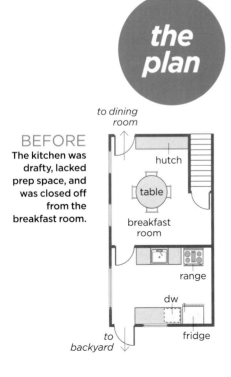

BEFORE
The kitchen was drafty, lacked prep space, and was closed off from the breakfast room.

to dining room

hutch

table

breakfast room

range

dw

fridge

to backyard

1 **REMOVED THE WALL** separating the kitchen and breakfast room.

2 **ADDED AN ISLAND** to provide a large prep surface.

3 **MOVED THE SINK** to the rear wall, under a new casement window with views of the backyard.

to dining room

hutch

island

fridge

range

dw

to backyard

4 **REORIENTED THE BASEMENT DOOR** so it lines up with the fridge cabinet.

5 **EXPOSED RAFTERS** in the existing kitchen space, adding rigid-foam insulation and drywall between them.

6 **RELOCATED THE RANGE** to a side wall and added a hood with a vent pipe narrow enough to fit between rafters.

the details

→ **THE ORIGINAL HUTCH** was updated with paint and nickel latches and pulls.

↓ **BLACK WALNUT PLANKS** in random widths now unite the space underfoot.

↑ **THE PANELED DOOR** to the dining room was a keeper, as was the original breakfast-room wainscot.

↑ **THE ISLAND** gets its character from the reclaimed fir's rich patina, finished with mineral oil.

EASY UPGRADE

Find reclaimed wood at salvage stores and have it cut to fit, then sanded and sealed to add one-of-a-kind character to a standard island base.

← **WHITE DISPLAY SHELVES** open up the space above the fridge and hold wine and decorative items.

An extra-thick butcher-block top balances the heft of the island.

before
The disjointed, L-shaped kitchen offered sadly little prep space and a jumbled decor.

LIGHT WITH DARK

PROBLEM> The kitchen suffered from a hodge-podge layout and no real prep space.
SOLUTION> Square off the room to accommodate a wealth of colorful cabinets and wide expanses of countertop.

WHEN YOU FALL IN LOVE WITH A HOUSE for its great character, remodeling is a matter of helping new spaces live in harmony with old ones. At least that's how the owners of this 1866 Italianate home regarded the renovation of its woefully outdated kitchen. The couple and their three daughters lived in the house for 10 long years before tackling a major overhaul that included bumping out the kitchen and adding an adjacent laundry room. By then, they knew exactly what they wanted. Their wish list included more storage and meal-prep space and a big dose of vintage style, including a spot for the rebuilt 1930s stove that the husband purchased from an online auction site and drove home from three states away.

Today, the sun-filled kitchen includes long expanses of honed black-granite and butcher-block countertops, and room to hang out, making the kitchen the family's go-to spot. White walls recede against sunny-yellow Shaker-style cabinets that reinforce the old-house character the family sought. A black island, with the hickory flooring, balances the bright room. As the husband concludes, "It finally feels right, like having a part of the house that was always missing."

after
The kitchen mixes high performance with vintage charm, thanks to yellow cabinets and a 1930s stove.

The chrome-trimmed range hood was custom made to match the vintage stove. ↓

PENDANT LIGHTING in white glass and chrome helps unify the modern stainless-steel fridge and the vintage stove.

the plan

AFTER

By adding and subtracting space, the kitchen became nearly square. It's smaller by a few square feet, but more workable thanks to repositioned appliances.

BEFORE

The L-shaped kitchen was poorly laid out. The range and the fridge had no adjacent landing space; the room lacked prep area.

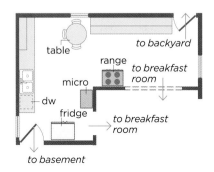

1 **BUMPED OUT** the sink wall several feet to create a step-saving layout, and added a pair of windows over the basins.

2 **ADDED A STORAGE ISLAND** that hides a microwave and doubles as a table.

3 **MOVED THE RANGE AND FRIDGE** to create an efficient work triangle, and flanked the range with prep counters.

4 **TRIMMED THE L,** donating that space to a new laundry room next door.

5 **WIDENED AN OPENING** to the breakfast room for better flow. A basement door was removed, and a new entry leads to the hall.

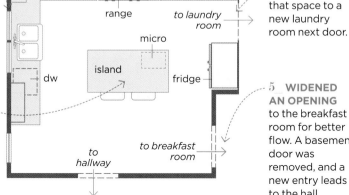

the details

↓**REPRODUCTION SCHOOLHOUSE LIGHTS** reinforce the period look.

↑**OLD-FASHIONED LATCHES** on the topmost cabinets let doors close with an evocative click. Their silvery finish provides visual continuity with the appliances.

→**THE BRIDGE FAUCET** is a graceful counterpoint to the chunky sink. The sink cabinet's feet echo those on the stove; hickory flooring grounds the yellow cabinetry.

✳ TOH DESIGN ADVICE
Add windows if you can. It not only makes a space more pleasant, it reduces the need for artificial light, lowering your power usage.

←**A REBUILT 1930S RANGE** is flanked by Shaker-style cabinets with chrome bin pulls and knobs.

↑**NEW WINDOWS** were trimmed to match others in the house and painted to blend in with the white subway tile for a seamless effect that enhances the room's feeling of spaciousness.

IDEA FILE

A hit of color can turn the functional elements in a room into eye-catching focal points. Cabinets make a statement that you can play up or tone down with your choice of hue. Walls and ceilings lend themselves to clever treatments with paint or paper. Here are more colorful ideas for transforming your kitchen space.

↑ **INTRODUCE MULTIPLE COLORS** Here's the 60-30-10 rule in action, balancing multiple colors. Gray-green paint on cabinetry provides a unifying 60 percent base color in this kitchen. Blue, which accounts for 30 percent, highlights the center island. Red paint on the dining table and yellow on the cabinet doors' window trim add cheery accents for the last 10 percent.

← REVERSE THE CONVENTIONAL SCHEME
Paint cabinets and moldings a slightly darker shade of the wall color to create a subtle and sophisticated monochromatic scheme. The indigo-blue island balances the greenish gold of the overall room.

↓ USE WALLPAPER TO LINK THE FLOOR TO THE CEILING
Checked paper overhead adds more depth and liveliness than plain old paint, and costs a lot less than a similarly striking coffered treatment. Latex floor enamel covers worn wood planks, creating a cool contrast with white cabinetry.

→ PAINT THE CEILING THE DOMINANT COLOR
The lush green ceiling is unconventional, to be sure. But surrounded by neutrals it gives the overall space a more finished look. A terra-cotta tile floor has the same intensity of color to balance the effect.

→ **LET WALLPAPER SET THE SCHEME** Make a lively floral wallpaper the starting point for a color scheme. Pull out colors such as yellow for this tin ceiling and green for the wainscoting. A white background for the stove opposite the white island keeps the dramatic expanses of color from feeling overwhelming.

↓ **MAKE A STRIKING STATEMENT WITH TILE** In an enclosed area, such as a backsplash behind a sink or a stove, a concentrated use of patterned tile is a thrifty way to introduce striking color in an otherwise white space. These graphic cement floor tiles fit together like puzzle pieces to form bright medallions.

＊ TOH DESIGN ADVICE

Neighbors on the color wheel, like this yellow and green, create a harmonious effect when put together. Opposites on the wheel, like green and red, deliver a more vibrant punch.

← FOCUS ON THE ISLAND Painted schoolhouse red, this island becomes the kitchen's visual anchor. Red accents, like ceramic bowls displayed in glass-front Shaker-style cabinets, help unify the room.

↓ PUNCH UP THE APPLIANCES
The vibrant turquoise hue of these vintage-style appliances puts a fresh spin on a simple white kitchen. A tumbled-glass backsplash carries the color around the room.

→ **DRAW ATTENTION TO DETAILS** Brights enhance a kitchen's laid-back vibe and put some of the focus on custom pieces, including a window-mounted plate rack and extra-long island. Symmetrical placement of colors—twin green window frames with twin red plate racks and striped curtains, blue cabinets on adjacent walls—helps create a feeling of harmony. A wood-topped red island anchors the space.

✳ TOH DESIGN ADVICE

Pairing bold colors? Use white in between, for trim or on a wall, so colors can shine alone as well as together.

←**TIE TOGETHER THE WALLS AND THE FLOOR** Sunny-yellow walls highlight glass-front cabinets with red trim applied to glass-panel doors. A cheerful checkerboard vinyl-tile floor and vintage linoleum rug pull it all together. For an extra dose of fun, mix in character-filled flea-market finds.

→**CREATE DRAMA WITH COMPLEMENTARY COLORS** Mint-green and deep-plum cabinets go together when treated with the same brown-tinted glaze. Greenish-brown limestone countertops and mossy-brown painted shelves provide a link to the wood ceiling beams.

EXPOSED CEILING TIMBERS, a butcher-block work surface, and a pot rack overhead give this state-of-the-art kitchen, with its secondhand restaurant range, farmhouse cred. A henhouse and vegetable patch are just outside the two-part Dutch door.

CHAPTER 6

THE FARMHOUSE KITCHEN

What gives a cook space a homey, rustic feel? A big worktable and an apron-front sink. A mix of cabinets and cupboards that look like they've been refreshed a few times with a coat of paint. Pots and dishes stored out in the open. Warm wood beams overhead and well-worn planks underfoot. Keep it simple, and see how easily hardworking stainless steel can fit in. Read on for more stylish updates to this look that feels so comfortable and familiar—even if you've never set foot on a farm.

before +afters

1_ **Bump Out in Back**

2_ **One Room for All**

3_ **Mix Don't Match**

The kitchen's showpiece, a vintage white-enameled range, was crammed in one corner.

before

BUMP OUT IN BACK

PROBLEM> A long-ago remodel left a kitchen out of step with the house's origins and its present needs. **SOLUTION>** Expand the room with a small addition, keeping its farm-fresh personality intact.

WHEN IT COMES TIME TO TACKLE A MAJOR PROJECT, who doesn't leave the hardest part till the end? After seven years of living in an 1880s farmhouse, these homeowners finally faced up to a kitchen overhaul. They had bought the fixer-upper on five overgrown acres from a widow who had lived there since 1917. The kitchen, they figured, was probably last touched in the 1940s, when the white-enameled range was installed.

In order to design an addition that would allow for an expanded cooking and eating space, the wife called on her architect sister. The vision was to retain as much of the kitchen's original character as possible while pushing out walls to include a larger dining area, a computer desk, room for the refrigerator that was stashed in the mudroom, and plenty of custom storage cabinets given an aged look with a distressed paint finish. Keepers included the existing 10-foot ceiling, fir floors (which were discovered under vinyl), existing entrances to the dining room and mudroom, and, of course, the old gas range that had become part of the family. "It belongs in this house," says the wife. And now, so does the entire kitchen.

With a plate rack over the sink, painted flat-panel cabinets, and an island that resembles a farm table, the renovated kitchen has a period look that blends with the rest of the 1880s house.

after

Try turning a ready-made table into an island with a platform base and bun feet.

Even basic 4-by-4-inch tiles can be effective with a few bright 2-by-2s mixed in. →

→ **THE EXISTING VINTAGE RANGE** is now centered on the long wall of the expanded kitchen, becoming the focal point the homeowners wanted. The new exhaust hood is paneled to match the rest of the woodwork, and is flanked by upper cabinets that keep cooking supplies close by.

the plan

BEFORE

Counter space was limited mostly to the drainboard. Appliances were split between two rooms; the fridge was out in the mudroom.

↑ *to dining room*

range

table

to mudroom →

AFTER

Twice its original size after bumping out the former range wall, the kitchen now holds all the appliances as well as an island and a dining table.

1 **ADDED WORK SURFACES** to the entire length of the new range wall. The countertop to the right of the sink was made deeper. An island also provides prep space.

2 **RECONFIGURED THE WINDOWS** with double-hungs on either side of the range. Two more windows were installed on the back wall to brighten the eating area.

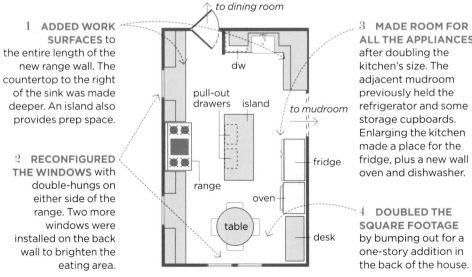

↑ *to dining room*

dw

pull-out drawers   island

to mudroom →

range

fridge

oven

table

desk

3 **MADE ROOM FOR ALL THE APPLIANCES** after doubling the kitchen's size. The adjacent mudroom previously held the refrigerator and some storage cupboards. Enlarging the kitchen made a place for the fridge, plus a new wall oven and dishwasher.

4 **DOUBLED THE SQUARE FOOTAGE** by bumping out for a one-story addition in the back of the house.

the details

↓ **THE NEW EATING AREA** is double the size of the old one and features a pedestal table with four chairs. The bumpout also made room for a desk to accommodate the family computer.

← **THE PINE ISLAND,** topped with the same garnet-veined gray granite as the countertops, was inspired by a thick-legged table the homeowner saw in a furniture-shop window.

EASY UPGRADE

Having an island built? Consider customizing it with work and storage options, such as a slide-out cutting board and wire-front drawers for produce.

→ **THE 1940S "DUAL-FUEL" RANGE,** which can be fired up with gas, wood, or coal, worked like new after the homeowners disassembled it and boiled the parts to degrease them. Its two-piece flip-up enamel cooktop cover provides extra workspace when folded down.

↑ **THE APRON-FRONT SINK,** leaded-glass cabinet doors, and custom-built cherry plate-drying rack look like they could be original to the 1880s farmhouse.

↑ Outfit an island with one or two electrical outlets so that you can run small appliances there.

A puny blue kitchen from the 1960s offered no room to move, let alone prepare a meal.

ONE ROOM FOR ALL

PROBLEM> A larger kitchen was in order, but the small-house footprint could not expand.
SOLUTION> Join three rooms to turn the first floor into one big space, then add age-old charm with a combination of materials.

IT'S THE DOWNSIDE of living in a 200-year-old farmhouse: small rooms, no storage space, and, of course, a teeny kitchen. With five kids and a passion for cooking, the wife really wanted—and needed—decent food-prep space. "Could we knock down the dining room wall?" she asked her husband, even showing him a floor plan she'd sketched out. He blanched, noting that he'd seen other old homes get cut up and ruined. Though he had put on a small addition soon after buying the house, he never wanted to alter the old home's interior. But weeks after that first sketch, the wife queried again with a second one: "What if we took down the living room wall, too?" That would potentially quadruple the size of the kitchen and allow for designated areas for meal prep, eating, and relaxing, plus tons of storage.

The idea was radical but smart, and the husband realized it might be their best route to a large kitchen. To help the new space slip easily into its shell of heart-pine floors and exposed fir ceilings, circa 1797, their kitchen designer specified three cabinet finishes reminiscent of the colonial era: heavily distressed sapphire-blue and black painted wood, and a natural mahogany stain. Now enjoying the expansive new space, the husband wonders aloud, "Why didn't we have the courage to do this sooner?"

after

A mix of cabinet finishes and an open plan anchored by a large L-shaped island give this kitchen its 18th-century-farmhouse appeal.

The range hood is hidden behind a stucco shell that was trimmed out with salvaged timbers.

AN EXPOSED WOOD CEILING reinforces the farmhouse feel; cable lighting appears to float between the timbers. A colonial-style chandelier keeps the look authentic.

BEFORE
The existing kitchen was closed off from the living and dining rooms.

the plan

AFTER
Two interior walls were removed to quadruple the size of the kitchen and create one big cooking, eating, and living space anchored by a large island.

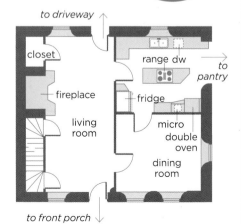

to driveway

closet

range dw

to pantry

fireplace

fridge

living room

micro double oven

dining room

to front porch

3 ESTABLISHED COOKING AND EATING ZONES with a partial wall next to the range that defines the work area in the open-plan kitchen.

1 DESIGNATED LOUNGING AREAS around the fireplace; nearby is a wet bar.

to driveway

wet bar

micro

closet

wine cooler

kids' fridge

to pantry

post

range

island

prep sink

fireplace

granite

butcher block

dw

to front porch

fridge

2 INSTALLED BUTCHER BLOCK on the island for food prep and a granite top for casual dining.

4 ADDED COUNTER SPACE, a range, and a fridge to one blank wall and a sink and dishwasher to another to create a work triangle.

the details

→ **THE WET BAR,** with handy access to the coffeemaker and the wine cooler on either side of the bar sink, doubles as the kids' snack corner, with a second fridge set next to a child-height microwave.

→ **VARYING CABINET COLORS** makes the kitchen look like it was added onto over time. The island's cherry cabinets were painted sapphire and black, then heavily distressed. Other cabinets were stained mahogany.

Soapstone counters run right up to windows in thick stone walls. ↓

↑ **THE BASE OF THE ISLAND** is packed with storage, including recessed cabinets under the seating counters.

← **THE SOAPSTONE SINK** was ordered deeper (25 inches) and wider (3 feet) than anything the homeowners could find in a showroom. It was also designed with a slanted front.

EASY UPGRADE

Add drainage grooves to a stone, concrete, or solid-surface countertop to give it old-fashioned charm. They eliminate puddling when pots are being washed and dried by hand.

The room was cramped, dark, and nondescript, with no place to sit for meals.

MIX DON'T MATCH

PROBLEM> Small and dark, the kitchen felt unappealing and out of sync with the old house.
SOLUTION> Expand the space to allow for better work flow, add a dining area, and incorporate storage pieces with a furniture look.

OLD HOUSE IN NEED OF NEW KITCHEN. It's as problematic as it is familiar, especially if you're like the homeowner-architect who wanted to preserve the aesthetic of this late-19th-century house while building a state-of-the-art cooking space. His solution: Mix it up, which is what he and his wife did when they enlarged the kitchen in the side-hall Colonial Revival to create a look that would be compatible with the original era of the house. They began by discreetly bumping out the existing dark, cramped kitchen. "Putting an addition on the side limited square footage but was more in keeping with the house than building out to the rear with a great room and a deck," says the husband.

Inside, the goal was an eclectic look that suggested that the kitchen had evolved with the house: a blend of furniture pieces and built-ins with different paint and stain finishes—and a commercial range. To integrate all of this, the kitchen designer hired custom cabinetmakers and specified stone and copper countertops, ebonized oak floors, and a subway-tile backsplash that covered the whole wall, as it would have in a house of this era. "Now," says the husband, "when people come to visit, they ask, 'Where's the addition?'"

after

The kitchen looks like it evolved over decades, thanks to the combination of a cherry bookcase, a green-painted prep-sink cabinet, raised-panel upper cabinets, and distressed-white built-ins.

A wall sconce in the window-seat alcove provides light for nighttime reading.

→**THE SINK** was relocated to the short wall that faces the backyard. This also freed up the adjacent wall for a range between two long stretches of countertop.

EASY UPGRADE
Give a cabinet added function—and vintage appeal—with a plate rack. These are available as an option from many manufacturers and also as kits, so you can add one yourself.

Cabinets with a curved corner are copies of a set in the kitchen of the homeowner's grandmother.

the plan

AFTER
The expanded floor plan more than doubled the space. The eating area connects to the new kitchen near the relocated sink, saving steps during cleanup.

BEFORE
The kitchen was particularly awkward due to a range placed in the center of the room.

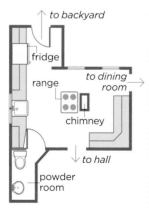

1 **REMOVED THE OLD SINK WALL** to make way for a rectangular addition.

2 **RELOCATED THE APPLIANCES** to create an efficient galley workspace. The range forms a triangle with the prep sink and fridge.

3 **REASSIGNED AUXILIARY SPACES** for better use. The kitchen's back entry became a mini mudroom. The old powder room was turned into a pantry.

4 **CREATED AN EATING AREA** where the old kitchen had been; now it holds a large table and chairs.

5 **MADE DEEP SILLS FOR DISPLAY** by bumping out windows more than 1 foot. The third bumpout hosts a window seat.

the details

↓ A WINDOW SEAT is at one end of the kitchen next to a bookcase with the wife's cookbook collection. The cherry top is curved out for comfort. Painted paneling on the base echoes that above the range hood.

← THE PREP-SINK CABINET has a copper countertop with an integral basin, copper-plated faucets, and pull-out produce baskets below. Its color, and that of the walls, was inspired by a vintage tackle box used as a bread box (to the right of the sink).

↓ THE EATING AREA occupies the old kitchen's work zone. The homeowners liked the exposed brick of the boiler chimney and filled in the adjacent wall with a cherry filing cabinet and shelves.

↑ ETCHED FROSTED GLASS marks the entry to the pantry. The tackboard, chalkboard, and mini desk were framed by the cabinetmaker to match built-ins.

SMART SAVE

Turn an old cabinet door into a message center by priming the panel surfaces with two coats of magnetic paint followed by a coat of chalkboard paint.

← PIERCED-TIN CABINET DOORS are reminiscent of a pie safe and add textural interest.

USING ALL SOLID-PANEL DOORS rather than adding in some with glass fronts keeps contents under wraps for a seamless, unified look. A second set of uppers is handy for stowing occasional-use or seasonal serving dishes.

CHAPTER 7>

THE HIDE-EVERYTHING KITCHEN

The kitchen is a classic clutter magnet. Not only because everyone passes through—depositing keys, sunglasses, backpacks, and unpaid bills along the way—but because it usually holds lots of specialized gear, from small appliances to cooking gadgets to all manner of pots and pans. Then there are the groceries, cleaning supplies, and bulk buys to deal with. The ideas on the upcoming pages will help you create a space that's a model of organization, both inside and outside the cabinet box.

before +afters

Besides providing a big prep area, the island houses a dishwasher, pull-out recycling bins, and cabinet and drawer storage for cookware and utensils. On the island's other side, the walnut counter extends an extra foot to provide space for stools and knees.

MULTIPLE PANTRIES

PROBLEM> A couple craved a sunny, open kitchen but also had a lot to store.
SOLUTION> Use white cabinets stacked to the ceiling and smart built-ins to create maximum storage while brightening a small space.

WITH ITS WALNUT-TOPPED ISLAND, marble counters, and wide white oak floorboards, the room is elegant, to be sure. But its real beauty lies in much more than a pretty face. With twin sinks, two dishwashers, double wall ovens, a warming drawer, a 48-inch range, a full-size refrigerator, a full-size freezer, and cabinets, cabinets, and more cabinets, this is one high-functioning facility for cooking, cleaning up, and—above all—storing. Tucked between a breakfast room and a large, oval dining room, the kitchen is, in fact, relatively small. But the homeowners have maximized storage while keeping the room bright with an expanse of windows over the sinks. "In today's kitchens, storage needs exceed workspace needs," says the couple's architect.

"The kitchen's extremely functional," says the husband, who worked with the architect on the details, then hired a firm known for its precision boat interiors to build the white-painted, raised-panel maple cabinets. Care was taken to specify interior features to keep the acres of stored items in order. A pull-out bin holds recycling containers; a blind-corner base cabinet has slide-over, swing-out shelves; drawer dividers organize spices, and a sliding library ladder makes the topmost cupboards accessible. In a world where having too much storage is almost unheard of, this couple has it good. "There's so much cupboard space," says the husband, "we'll probably never fill it up."

False fronts help conceal many appliances, → including a dishwasher.

→ **RAISED PANELS** help conceal the kitchen's multiple appliances, like the trash compactor located between the sinks.

↓ **UPPER CABINETS** accessible by ladder extend to the 10-foot ceiling, providing storage for little-used gear.

Pilasters between banks of windows break up the expanse of glass.

BEFORE + AFTER

the plan

Plenty of pantries, cabinets, and drawers provide storage in this kitchen. Twin sinks, a range, and a full-size fridge form a compact work triangle. Multiple appliances allow each workstation to handle prep and cleanup for a crowd.

1 **ADDED TWO PANTRIES** just outside the kitchen to store items not needed for cooking.

2 **LOCATED THE RANGE** on its own wall, with landing space on either side.

3 **BUILT IN A TALL PANTRY** next to the recessed kitchen office to provide symmetry in a space chockablock with storage.

4 **INSTALLED AN ISLAND** to get more space for work and storage. Stool seating hosts breakfast and casual meals.

5 **DOUBLED UP ON SINKS** and dishwashers to save steps during cleanup.

cleaning/kitchen supplies pantry

food pantries

desk

cookware pantry

to breakfast room

glassware pantry

to hall

recycling bins

paper goods pantry

ovens/ tray storage

dw

fridge

freezer

dw

trash compactor

linen storage/ warming drawer

range

to dining room

the details

↓**A PANTRY** devoted to pots and pans keeps them out of sight but readily accessible.

EASY UPGRADE
U-shaped shelves put the entire contents of a storage cabinet on view. Rounded corners make scrapes less likely.

↑**COOKING SUPPLIES** are stored close by in a cabinet in the range-side storage wall; shelves are spaced well apart to fit tall bottles.

↑**A CUSTOM-MADE LIBRARY LADDER** that slides along a metal track helps to access items stowed on high.

←**VERTICAL DIVIDERS** made of plywood and located beneath the ovens organize baking sheets and trays; recessed edges make stored items easy to grab.

before

HIDDEN ASSETS

PROBLEM> The stripped-down kitchen barely had a place to put away a single pot.
SOLUTION> Nearly triple the size of the room by adding on, then line the walls with crisp white doors and drawers that hide modern conveniences.

THERE'S AN ART TO OPENING UP an old house. Sure, those small hallways and rooms can feel like back alleys and dead ends, but get carried away during demolition and you may sacrifice charm along with the original butler's pantry.

The designer of this kitchen, known for his work on historic houses, likes to solve this problem by cutting and pasting with care while honoring period details. To introduce flow to the 1908 foursquare, he added on in back, nearly tripling the kitchen's size. Then he salvaged and matched the butler's pantry cabinets and woodwork, and gave the new space a clean, buttoned-down look. "We have two kids, so there is always stuff around, but it never feels cluttered," says the wife, who stashes bills on a desk tucked inside a drop-front cabinet (a TV nearby is hidden similarly). A microwave and smaller appliances also sit behind retractable doors. Barn-red walls, an oak floor, and a tawny beadboard ceiling warm up a room lined in vintage white. "People come in," says the wife, "and don't know it's new."

after

Bigger and brighter, the kitchen has tons of storage and workspace, including a peninsula with a perch for helpers.

Stained beadboard warms up the high-ceilinged, mostly white space.

Flush-to-the-counter cabinets were wired to hide a TV and small appliances.
↓

↑WALL-TO-WALL CABINETS keep the kitchen shipshape.

the plan

BEFORE
The kitchen was too small for a table or an island, and was walled off from the original butler's pantry.

to hallway →

range

work-table

broom closet

flue

dw

to butler's pantry →

fridge

closet

AFTER
Now almost three times larger, the narrow room holds an easy-to-navigate-around peninsula plus a breakfast area and ample storage.

1 EXTENDED THE ROOM, allowing space for a light-filled breakfast area and more-fluid traffic.

2 ADDED A PENINSULA, providing prep space and a snack bar.

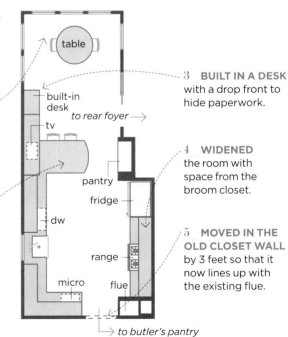

table

built-in desk

tv

to rear foyer →

pantry

fridge

dw

range

micro

flue

to butler's pantry →

3 BUILT IN A DESK with a drop front to hide paperwork.

4 WIDENED the room with space from the broom closet.

5 MOVED IN THE OLD CLOSET WALL by 3 feet so that it now lines up with the existing flue.

the details

↓ **NEW WINDOW CASING** and crown molding were based on existing trim in the 1908 house.

← **BLACK GRANITE COUNTERTOPS** provide a graphic counterpoint to cabinets, an apron-front sink, subway tile, and trim paint all in crisp white.

EASY UPGRADE

In a kitchen with lots of cabinets, add window shutters in the same finish to maintain an unbroken visual line and make the room appear more open.

→ **V-GROOVE PANELING** on the range hood echoes the wainscoting. Satin-nickel latches and bin pulls reinforce the period look.

↑ **A FLIP-UP CABINET DOOR** slides back to reveal the microwave. To its left is a passageway to the butler's pantry, where cabinets—made to match the pantry originals—hide recycling bins.

A narrow kitchen was cut off from the dining room: When guests stood at the peninsula, they blocked the fridge.

before

CEILING-HIGH STORAGE

PROBLEM> **A 1980s kitchen didn't suit its 1930s house and was devoid of both style and storage.** SOLUTION> **Re-create vintage features with Shaker-style cabinets and a library ladder, concealing appliances and improving function.**

WHEN YOU WORK ALL DAY IN A HIGH-TECH JOB, it's nice to come home to a warm, nostalgia-inducing kitchen. But don't let this one's old-fashioned touches fool you. While the house was built circa 1930, the kitchen dated to the 1980s with a locked-in layout to prove it: When one person was rummaging in the fridge, no one else could navigate between it and the nearby peninsula to reach the eating area. With major ambitions and a micro-budget, the couple went strictly DIY. Bit by bit, they mapped out an open plan in which all the modern conveniences would be hidden. "It's an old house, and we both like older things," says the husband, an electrical engineer.

The first step was taking down the wall that separated the cramped kitchen from the adjacent dining room. Next the husband built and painted the Shaker-style cabinets, as well as false fronts that camouflage the fridge, trash compactor, microwave, and dishwasher. He also constructed an island that holds the range; in addition, it serves as a prep space and divides the kitchen from the dining room, with cabinets that open on both sides. Three big ideas set the stage: those cabinets, a rolling ladder originally designed to gain access to library shelves, and a freestanding oak Hoosier cabinet base that evokes early unfitted kitchens. Once these were in place, more old-house touches the couple loves were added, from subway tiles and a twin-basin farmhouse sink to a wall-mount faucet and oil-rubbed bronze hardware. Kids and friends love the kitchen too, now that it's a place where everyone can comfortably gather.

after

Relocating the fridge to a far corner freed the peninsula for socializing. False fronts hide all the appliances except the stove.

Exposed icebox hinges lend a lot of charm to a lone upper cabinet.

↓**AN APRON-FRONT SINK** with twin basins became a period-appropriate centerpiece, complemented by old-fashioned subway tiles and a wall-mount faucet.

AFTER

Took down a wall to open up the kitchen to the dining room, and replaced it with an island that now holds the stove. Relocated the fridge to ease traffic at the peninsula.

↑**A ROLLING LIBRARY LADDER** accesses the topmost cabinets. After careful research, the couple found one they liked from a company that has been making them for over 100 years.

the plan

BEFORE

The space for the kitchen table was too cramped for a family of five. A lack of storage meant some cooking gear was stowed in the basement.

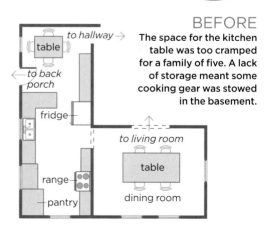

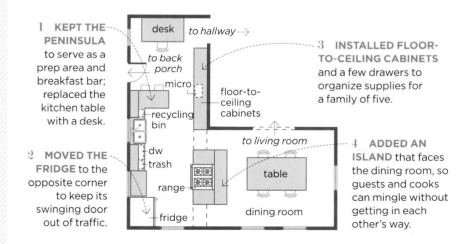

1 **KEPT THE PENINSULA** to serve as a prep area and breakfast bar; replaced the kitchen table with a desk.

2 **MOVED THE FRIDGE** to the opposite corner to keep its swinging door out of traffic.

3 **INSTALLED FLOOR-TO-CEILING CABINETS** and a few drawers to organize supplies for a family of five.

4 **ADDED AN ISLAND** that faces the dining room, so guests and cooks can mingle without getting in each other's way.

the details

Small cabinets over the island hug the ceiling and run wall to wall. →

→ A BI-LEVEL ISLAND replaced the wall, uniting kitchen and dining room while keeping the two spaces separate. The stove remains in the original location, eliminating the need to run a new line for gas.

↑ FREESTANDING FURNITURE typifies an era before built-in cabinets. A salvaged oak Hoosier cabinet base topped with butcher block becomes a versatile secondary workstation. Next to it, granite countertops feature a honed finish to look like soapstone, minus the maintenance.

→ THE FRIDGE resembles an old-fashioned pantry. The homeowner found a salvaged door, cut it in half, and planed it to reduce the weight. Then he used screws and wood strips to create cleats to attach it. The front is fitted with a door handle.

✳ TOH DESIGN ADVICE If you have more wall space than floor space, opt for shallow, to-the-ceiling cabinets. You'll get plenty of storage with no need for costly interior pull-outs.

IDEA FILE

You may have plenty of deep cabinets in your kitchen, but without some well-thought-out helpers, you're only halfway to getting organized. Achieve more efficient use of your space with storage ideas that make it easy to stow—and retrieve—every item.

→ **PULLOUT PILASTER**
One of the most under-utilized spaces in many kitchens is the gap between cabinets and appliances such as the dishwasher or range. Here, a pull-out pilaster reveals a rack for hanging dish towels; similar pull-outs can also be fitted with shelves for spices or hooks for oven mitts.

↓ **INTEGRAL KNIFE BLOCK**
Free up some counter space by storing your blades in a drawer with protective wood slots. Graduated sizes accommodate big carvers as well as little parers.

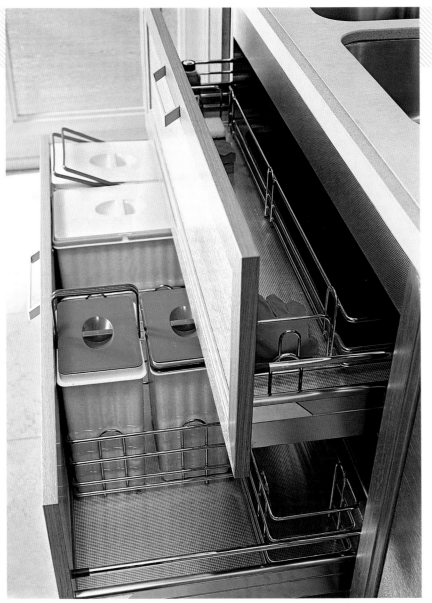

← UNDER-SINK ORGANIZER

That no-man's land of pipes, trash cans, and random cleaning supplies beneath the sink is where even the most organized among us can go astray. These drawers can change all that, with compartments for sponges and scouring pads in the U-shaped unit on top, and space for cleaning products and recycling bins on the bottom.

↑ VENTED DRAWERS

Aside from adding visual texture, these wire-mesh-front cabinet drawers allow air to circulate, so you can use them to stash onions, potatoes, flour, and other items that require a cool, dark place.

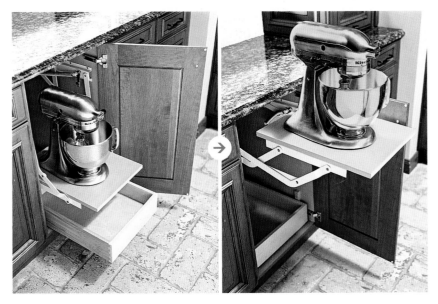

← POP-UP SHELF

If you don't use an appliance every day, why let it monopolize precious counter space (or, worse, get buried deep in cabinets where you have to excavate to find it)? This pop-up shelf is strong enough to support large items like stand mixers and blenders. A release mechanism allows to you gently push it back down when you're finished.

How to get organized

TIPS FROM
COLETTE SCANLON,
TOH DESIGN EDITOR

Of course, lots of cabinet space won't solve your storage problems unless you can find what you want when you want it. Here are some ideas to help you get your cooking essentials organized.

1 Store like things together: dishes with dishes, utensils with utensils, food with food.

2 Store things nearest their point of use: Cooking gear should be near the stove, dishes and glasses near the dishwasher, plastic wrap and bags where you are most likely to actually cover the leftovers or make the sandwiches.

3 Place things you use every day within easy reach; put less-used items at the back of shelves or in topmost cupboards.

4 Keep the kitchen a kitchen; if you're short on space, store lightbulbs, tools, cleaning supplies, and pet food elsewhere.

5 Install lazy Susans in corners to make it easier to find jars and cans.

6 Screw in cup hooks under shelves to make use of otherwise wasted space.

7 Have a huge collection of plastic containers? They'll stay better organized nested in a drawer instead of stuck on a cabinet shelf.

8 Install racks for pot lids, spices, or canned goods on the insides of cabinet doors.

9 Equip base cabinets with pull-out shelves or bins to make the contents more accessible.

10 Pare down your kitchen possessions. If you haven't used something for a couple of years, maybe you don't need it at all.

← PEGBOARD DRAWER
Instead of having to heft plates onto hard-to-reach overhead shelves, you can stack them securely between adjustable pegs (round or triangular) in this deep base-cabinet drawer. An added bonus: The kids have no excuse not to help unload the dishwasher.

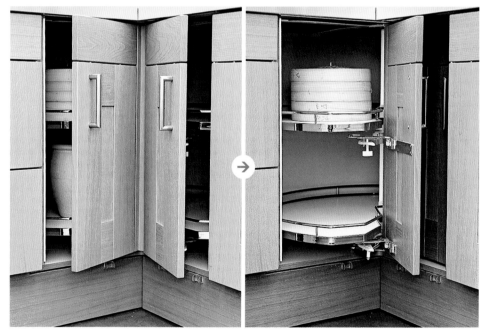

↑ TURNTABLE DOORS An improvement on an already good idea, this lazy Susan has doors that fold into each other when you rotate the carousel, giving you unfettered access to all the soup cans, cereal boxes, or bamboo steamers you need. When you're done, just give the carousel a whirl, and the doors pop back into place.

↓ STORE TO THE FLOOR

By taking advantage of the rarely used toekick under a base cabinet, this deceptively deep single drawer creates a new storage unit, where you can put large pots and pans, bags of dog food, or cases of bottled water.

↑ CUTLERY CARRYALL

So simple you wonder why somebody didn't think of it before. Putting handles on a utensil tray means you can carry it over to set the table or bring it to the dishwasher when unloading. Optional adjustable slots on the side let you create spaces for smaller items, like a corkscrew or a citrus reamer.

← SLIDING CORNER RACK

Inaccessible space, like a deep corner recess, is almost as annoying as no space at all. This hingeless door, backed by generous metal shelves, pulls out and swivels, clearing the way for a large rear basket to slide over, putting even the most deeply buried items within easy reach.

INSTALLING TWO FAUCETS—one at the sink and one over the range—ensures optimal convenience for an avid home chef. A large expanse of prep space eases multitasking. Sleek finishes keep the room looking its best even at its busiest.

CHAPTER 8
THE COOK'S KITCHEN

There are probably as many cooking styles as there are cooks. But every home chef can agree on this: You can always use a bit more storage and prep space, and an extra fridge, sink, or dishwasher would come in handy too. To design a kitchen that cooks as good as it looks, start with the work zone. It should function like a traffic cop, keeping everything and everyone moving safely. Once you have a plan, fill in with your favorite fixtures and finishes—or borrow some of the inspiring ideas in the examples ahead.

*before
+afters*

1_ **Separate Prep Areas**

2_ **Guests Welcome**

3_ **Tight Work Triangle**

The gloomy galley was far too small for a couple who like to cook together.

before

SEPARATE PREP AREAS

PROBLEM> A galley-style kitchen lacked room for even a dishwasher, let alone two devoted cooks. **SOLUTION>** Expand into adjoining spaces, then reconfigure the floor plan to create three distinct work zones.

THE CHEERY KITCHEN in this 1916 bungalow plays host to two serious cooks who like to cook together—a pleasure that their old, galley-style kitchen denied them. "It had never been updated, so there was no storage and no dishwasher—not even a place to eat," says the husband.

Working with an architect, they borrowed space from adjoining areas of the house to nearly double the kitchen's size. This cleared the way for three workstations, including a central island equipped with a range and breakfast bar. The husband, a woodworker, designed the white-painted custom cabinetry to fit the couple's needs and the era of their house, using flat-panel and glass-front doors, beadboard backing on some pieces, and brushed-nickel hardware. They then chose yellow walls to keep it sunny, night and day. "Our goal was to create an inviting, modern kitchen that suited the age of the house," says the husband. "And we love to entertain but hate to miss the party. This design lets us do both."

New French doors in the bigger, brighter kitchen open onto the porch. Left of the island is a prep area with a butcher-block top and a second sink. A built-in hutch in the corner serves as a baking center.

after

The extended tile backsplash protects the wall from food-prep spatters. →

→WHITE CUSTOM CABINETRY blends with a subway-tile backsplash for a period look—with high-end appliances. It's anchored by a central island, with a honed granite countertop, that houses a six-burner range, a microwave, storage on three sides, and a breakfast bar.

EASY UPGRADE

Adding a schoolhouse light over the sink or several in a row over an island is a sure way to inject vintage charm. Look for ceiling-mount styles as well as longer pendants that bring task lighting closer to a work surface.

the plan

AFTER

Almost double in size now, the kitchen gained space by claiming an adjoining closet, an unused chimney, part of the porch, and the basement stairs.

BEFORE

The dismal galley couldn't accommodate a couple of serious cooks.

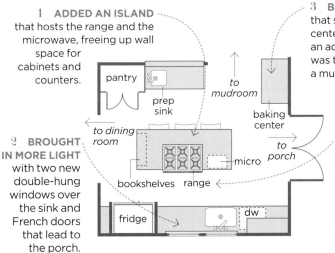

to bedroom

fridge

range

butcher block

to dining room

to porch

1 ADDED AN ISLAND that hosts the range and the microwave, freeing up wall space for cabinets and counters.

pantry

prep sink

to mudroom

3 BUILT A HUTCH that serves as a baking center. In the process, an adjoining bedroom was turned into a mudroom.

baking center

2 BROUGHT IN MORE LIGHT with two new double-hung windows over the sink and French doors that lead to the porch.

to dining room

bookshelves   range

micro

to porch

fridge

dw

4 TIGHTENED UP THE WORK TRIANGLE by placing the range in the island and the main sink and the refrigerator on the wall opposite.

the details

↓ **A BUTCHER-BLOCK-TOPPED BASE CABINET** is used for prepping vegetables and doubles as a drinks station. The sink is outfitted with a high-neck bar faucet.

Knives stay handy on a magnetic rack next to a secondary work area.
↓

↓ **A BUNGALOW-STYLE PLATE RAIL** spans upper cabinets above the new French doors, providing storage and display. Painted poplar corbels help support the 17-inch-deep MDF shelf. The clock is a 1930s reproduction.

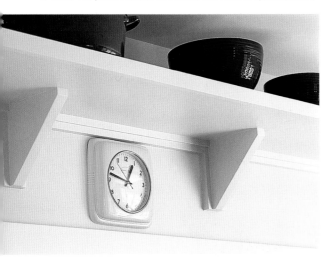

↑ **THE WALL-MOUNT BRIDGE FAUCET** with porcelain handles is a perfect complement to the original enameled cast-iron sink.

← **THE PANTRY,** like all the kitchen's cabinets, is made of paint-grade plywood with poplar trim and painted white. The top unit is outfitted with four deep shelves and additional shallow shelving on the doors; the base unit has pull-out shelves so that all contents are readily visible and accessible.

161

before

The old kitchen's Southwest look was a relic of a 1980s redo. The wide channel hiding the vent ductwork took up valuable space along the cooktop wall.

GUESTS WELCOME

PROBLEM> A serious cook's kitchen needed more storage, sizzle, and style for hosting frequent dinners. **SOLUTION>** Add pantry space, lots of burners, and a timeless design with warm-looking wood and tile.

WHEN COOKING IS MORE LOVE THAN LABOR, the kitchen often becomes party central. That was the case for the couple who remodeled this space—twice—to give the husband a suitable place to build his culinary skills. The first redo yielded a workable galley. But once he had plenty of prep space, the amateur chef decided the look of stock cabinets, countertops, and appliances was out of step with the four-course dinners he routinely prepared for his gourmet eating club. More storage space, a pro-grade range, and a handsome environment for both cooking and entertaining were all on the shopping list, but another space-reconfiguring remodel wasn't.

Luckily, the kitchen designer the couple brought in knew just how to boost storage while keeping the basic layout intact. He doubled the size of the pantry by breaking through an adjacent utility closet. He replaced existing cabinets along the walls and in the island and two peninsulas with Arts and Crafts–style cherry units, all customized inside with adjustable shelves of varying depths. After narrowing the over-the-range vent opening, he wrapped it with even more cabinets. The chef's reaction to the overhaul? Dinner guests can't visit often enough.

after

Classic Mission-style cabinetry warms up the new space. A narrower chimney for the vent hood allowed for extra storage cabinets on either side.

Terra-cotta tile makes for an easy-to-mop floor in a kitchen that sees a lot of cooking.
↓

→ **CABINETS AND DRAWERS** store frequently used pots and pans on the cook's side of the peninsula. On the opposite side, bookshelves display a collection of cookbooks.

EASY UPGRADE

In a room with lots of glazed wood cabinetry, treat all the wood surfaces the same way, from the door frames to the dining chairs, to give the space a unified look.

A peninsula provides the necessary landing space for double wall ovens. ↓

the plan

BEFORE + AFTER

The footprint and configuration remained the same except for the union of a pantry and utility closet to create one walk-in storage space concealed behind cabinetry panels. Eliminating a door swing also smoothed traffic flow.

1 **REDUCED THE VENT CHIMNEY** by 2 feet to allow a bit more room for upper cabinets over the grill and cooktop.

2 **CREATED AN "APPLIANCE WARDROBE"** out of a new partition and a same-size existing wall to enclose the fridge and convection ovens in the vaulted-ceilinged space. Cherry pilasters added to both sides give a finished look.

3 **DOUBLED THE PANTRY'S SIZE** by combining the existing pantry with an adjacent utility closet to create one large walk-in.

4 **CUSTOMIZED PANTRY STORAGE** with shelves for small appliances and cubbies for canned goods.

5 **INSTALLED BOOKSHELVES** on the side of the peninsula facing the eating area to hold cookbooks.

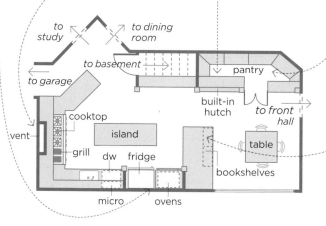

to study

to dining room

to basement

to garage

pantry

built-in hutch

to front hall

vent

cooktop

grill

island

dw

fridge

micro

ovens

bookshelves

table

the details

↓PILASTERS WITH RIBBON TRIM resulted from a collaboration between the kitchen designer and the couple; they were custom ordered from the cabinet company.

↑THE BUILT-IN KNIFE BLOCK was created from a slotted foot-long inset of canary wood and makes use of the 3 inches of dead space behind the base cabinets.

↑HONEY-COLOR GRANITE COUNTERS lighten up the cherry cabinets and are consistent with the Craftsman look.

EASY UPGRADE

When shopping for faucets and cabinet hardware, match finishes as closely as possible for the most polished look. Today a wide selection of tones and sheens is available, even within classic choices such as nickel and oil-rubbed bronze.

←LEADED-GLASS DOORS brighten the upper portion of the built-in hutch and suit the room's Arts and Crafts theme. They hide away bar glasses and stemware.

Stool slipcovers dress up a kitchen and bring the color scheme together.

A low ceiling, fussy wallpaper, and inadequate prep space made the dated kitchen feel cramped.

before

TIGHT WORK TRIANGLE

PROBLEM> A crowded cook space was ill-equipped for preparing meals, let alone welcoming guests.
SOLUTION> Annex a dining room and closet to double the size, then conceal all the appliances in cabinetry reminiscent of country antiques.

RENOVATIONS THAT BEGIN SMALL often have a way of growing. When an avid cook and her husband undertook the redo of the narrow kitchen in their 1960s raised ranch house, they mainly envisioned a fresh look and new appliances. But along the way, with a nudge from their architect and interior designer, the plan expanded.

To add height and length, the designer suggested raising the ceiling and absorbing the dining room (which would be relocated) to make way for a sitting area. She gave the kitchen a traditional "unfitted" look with linen-colored cabinets combined with a hutch and pantry in Provençal blue and a peninsula with a country-table profile. The size and heft of the storage pieces, which suggest antique furniture, make the up-to-date appliances—including a cooktop, double wall ovens, and a built-in side-by-side refrigerator—seem to disappear. Crown molding, cornices, and paneling unite the room and, together with wide-plank oak floors, a glass chandelier, and a comfy sofa, make the highly functional space a gathering place too. "Originally it wasn't planned for hanging out," says the wife. "Now it is."

after

Raising the ceiling, annexing adjacent spaces, and warming up the decor led to a more functional, inviting room for a cook who likes to have family and guests around her.

167

→ **CROWN MOLDING** on the cabinets, together with the strong horizontal lines of the mantel, help anchor the vaulted ceiling.

↓ **CERAMIC TILE BACKSPLASHES** inspired the color scheme. The tiles' varying shapes, sizes, and matte and glossy finishes add texture.

↑ Elaborate millwork details elevate the feel of the cooking space.

the plan

BEFORE
The small, low-ceilinged kitchen was hard to work in.

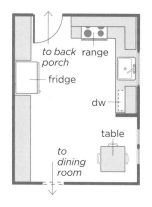

AFTER
Annexing the dining room nearly doubled the square footage and allowed for a hangout zone. The compact work triangle changed only slightly.

1 **INSTALLED A CUSTOM HUTCH** to store tableware and ground a peninsula that has drawers for spices and cutlery. The peninsula also provides extra prep space and a social hub.

2 **ANNEXED THE DINING ROOM,** allowing a better layout and room for a sitting area.

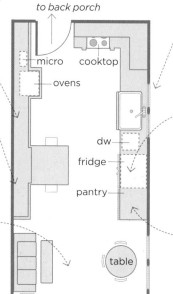

3 **REWORKED THE WINDOWS,** replacing one over the sink with two, closing up a pair to make room for the fridge and pantry, and replacing two in the former dining room.

4 **MOVED THE FRIDGE** to allow space for double wall ovens set into full-height cabinets. The sink and range kept their old spots to minimize plumbing hassles.

5 **PUT IN A PANTRY UNIT** to store provisions and to visually balance the hutch opposite it.

Wavy-glass fronts reinforce the built-in hutch's antique look.

← **THE BUILT-IN HUTCH,** made from custom cabinets, is integrated into the peninsula with a marble slab that provides a versatile additional workspace. Low stools preserve the open feel.

↑ **THE PANELED FRIDGE** has sculptural satin-nickel appliance pulls that add to its finished look.

→ **THE DEEP, FOOTED PANTRY** stores food and drinks, with small condiment bottles kept handy on shelves attached to the inside of one door. To its left is the fridge.

EASY UPGRADE

Replacing solid panels on a few cabinet doors with wire mesh evokes an old-fashioned pie safe and adds character to a kitchen.

↑ **TURNED LEGS,** a drawer with a bin pull, and a scalloped apron (which echoes trim on the hutch) give the hardworking peninsula table country-kitchen style.

WHITE-ON-WHITE makes for a sophisticated monochromatic scheme. Gray grout in the subway-tile backsplash and veining in the marble counters help keep the look soft rather than sterile.

CHAPTER 9 >

THE MOSTLY WHITE KITCHEN

Clean, fresh, bright. White helps make a kitchen look bigger and airier. It's also the most compatible partner for any other finish, making everything it comes close to look better: Woods are richer, colors more vibrant. Plus, its reflective qualities make the space feel sunny and welcoming throughout the day. White is versatile too: It works for any style of kitchen and allows you to update its look as often as you like for very little expense—just a few yards of fabric and some accessories. What's not to love?

before
+afters

171

Small, white-painted wood knobs recede into cabinetry for a clean look. →

The kitchen counter's deep corners were awkward to work in. Closed upper cabinets made the space feel cramped.

EFFICIENT GALLEY

PROBLEM> The 1960s U-shape layout was inefficient—and out of place in the 1740s home. **SOLUTION>** Move doorways, reconfigure as a galley, and add a bright-white period look.

SOMETIMES THE SIMPLE SOLUTION IS ALSO THE BEST, especially when righting past renovation wrongs. So thought one couple after seeking the advice of their architect in solving the layout and traffic-flow problems of their 1749 Dutch Colonial's kitchen. The kitchen was in a small, closed-off addition that was put on 100 years after the house was built, and it never quite fit in. To make matters worse, it was reconfigured in the 1960s as a U-shape with honey-hued cabinetry and marbleized-laminate counters. This made the space feel crowded and look dated—two big negatives for a couple whose social lives revolve around cooking for and entertaining friends.

The plan was straightforward: Bust out the bottom of the U to create an efficient galley with prep, cooking, and cleanup stations arrayed along two walls. By relocating the back door and enlarging the passageway into the adjoining living room so that the two line up, the homeowners were also able to open up the kitchen to both indoors and out, while routing foot traffic away from the main work zone. Now period details such as painted cabinets, soapstone counters, and an apron-front sink unite the space with the rest of the 18th-century farmhouse.

Two straight countertops offer more usable workspace. Open shelving makes the narrow galley appear more spacious and allows for displays of colorful dishware.

Picking the right white

TIPS FROM
COLETTE SCANLON,
TOH DESIGN EDITOR

1 Consider your other materials. The choices for surfaces and appliances should be compatible with the white you select. Want wood? Go with a warm white. Prefer stone? Then you will want to pair it with a cooler white that shares the same undertone.

2 Take sun exposure into account. Does the kitchen face north or south? Is sunlight stronger in the morning or afternoon? This, too, will influence your choice. Warm whites have a yellow undertone, cool whites a hint of green, blue, or gray.

3 Think about the mood you want to create. Do you want the overall effect to be expansive or cozy? Is the room rambling or small? As with any other color, warm whites will draw in walls, while cooler shades will make them recede.

SOAPSTONE COUNTERTOPS now run parallel on each long wall of the kitchen. Centering the stove allows for landing space on either side of the cooktop.

The contrast of a black pro-style range lends drama to white walls and cabinetry. →

the plan

AFTER
Moving the patio door and widening the entry to the living room created a direct path between indoors and out. The galley layout provides more usable counter space.

BEFORE
The U-shape layout was tight and the patio door's placement created traffic problems, with houseguests often traipsing through the work zone to get outside.

to patio

dw

range

fridge

to living room

walk-in pantry

1 MOVED THE EXTERIOR DOORWAY to be adjacent to a wall of storage, for a direct route from the living room to the patio.

2 INSTALLED FLOOR-TO-CEILING CABINETS in the space formerly occupied by a makeshift walk-in pantry.

3 RELOCATED THE SINK to the back wall to create a longer, unbroken expanse of soapstone countertop.

4 WIDENED THE PASSAGEWAY between the kitchen and the living room (the remaining column is structural).

5 RECESSED THE FRIDGE into a corner beside the built-ins so that houseguests can help themselves without entering the work zone.

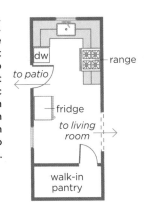

range

to living room
to patio

dw

micro   fridge

built-ins

pantry

the
details

→ **THE PANTRY BUILT-INS** are 2½ feet deep rather than the usual 2 feet, creating a flush look with the standard-depth refrigerator and providing extra stowing space.

↑ **A SLIDE-OUT STORAGE CUBE** holds cookbooks in the front and a built-in spice rack in the rear. A small microwave in the cubby below is usually hidden behind the cabinet's "flipper" doors, which open out into the room and then slide back neatly into recesses along the sides.

TOH DESIGN ADVICE

Think about using a wood floor to ground a sea of white—it is also easier on a cook's feet than a harder surface like tile or stone.

↑ **CABINET DIVIDERS** keep muffin tins and cookie sheets in upright order. The full-extension shelf above means no more kneeling and rooting around in a dark base cabinet for the right pot lid.

↑ **MAPLE CABINET DOORS,** with board-and-batten detail on the inside, conceal occasional-use serving pieces and wineglasses. Daily-use dishware is stacked on open shelving to either side of the sink.

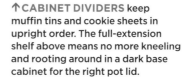

The kitchen was new, but someone else's vision. *before*

ZONE THE SPACE

PROBLEM> A kitchen designer's kitchen wasn't efficient—and wasn't her style.
SOLUTION> Mix white surfaces with wood to create a fresh look; approach multitasking thoughtfully to make the space super-functional.

EVER WONDER WHAT A KITCHEN DESIGNER'S dream kitchen looks like? For this homeowner, it doesn't have the carved-wood cabinets and glossy granite counters seen in so many showrooms. In fact, after moving into her traditional Colonial Revival, she stripped out just such a kitchen to put her stamp on the space. "It didn't reflect me, or the way I cook," says the designer, who prefers classic white cabinets with pale marble countertops, plus convenient drawer storage for everything from bread to blenders. A single sink and midrange appliances hadn't been optimal, either, for someone who loves to entertain, whether with a casual buffet, a sit-down dinner, or the occasional catered party.

So after gutting the room and selling its contents to a contractor, the owner set about maximizing every inch. She got rid of an awkward center support post by installing a steel beam, freeing up room for a larger island with a prep sink and seating. She specified pro-grade appliances throughout and simple white cabinets. Most important, now the cheerful space suits her aesthetic and lifestyle. "You don't need the most elaborate kitchen," says the designer, "just the one that you feel good in every day."

after

White cabinetry and pale marble countertops make the room bright. Mixed materials and varying heights turn the island into a multitasker; rich wood tones help draw the eye to this focal-point feature.

Divided-light windows, cabinet doors, and French doors unify the sink wall.

➜ THE STUDDED-STEEL HOOD and the six-burner cooktop with grill signal this is a serious cooking space.

↓ THE BLUE BOOKCASE INTERIOR provides a welcome dose of color amid long runs of white cabinetry.

↑ Install deep drawers below a cooktop for easy transfer of heavy cookware.

the plan

BEFORE

The kitchen lacked clear zones for cooking and eating.

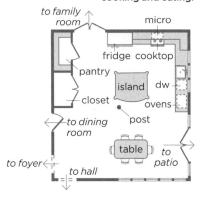

to family room
micro
fridge cooktop
pantry
island dw
closet
ovens
to dining room
post
to foyer
table
to patio
to hall

AFTER

Annexing a couple of feet from the family room and reconfiguring the pantry provided space to cluster the ovens. Removing a structural post made way for a larger island.

1 **ENLARGED THE FOOTPRINT SLIGHTLY,** taking a couple of feet from the family room to allow for a bigger, L-shaped pantry. An additional few feet grabbed from the dining room contributed to a new butler's pantry.

2 **ADDED AN ARCHED DOORWAY** where French doors had stood, as another way to encourage flow from the kitchen into the family room.

3 **INCREASED STORAGE** with 24-inch-deep drawers for baking supplies and food containers in the sides of the island that face the sink and the range.

4 **REWORKED THE ISLAND** and enlarged it. Where the butcher-block work surface graduates into a breakfast bar, its curved shape separates the eating zone from the cooking area.

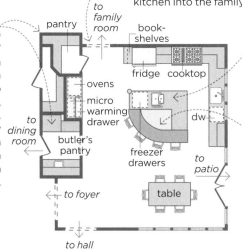

to family room
pantry
book-shelves
ovens
fridge cooktop
micro
warming drawer
to dining room
butler's pantry
dw
freezer drawers
to patio
to foyer
table
to hall

the details

→ **GLASS MOSAIC TILES** line a niche behind the range. The pattern reflects the green and blue accents in the room.

↓ **BEADBOARD ON THE SEATING SIDE** of the island hides three more cupboards. The island's other sides have drawers for utensils, dishes, and pots, plus two freezer drawers across from the refrigerator.

↑ **A TRIO OF COUNTER MATERIALS** addresses several functions: butcher block for food prep, marble for baking, butternut with a bronze stain for the breakfast bar.

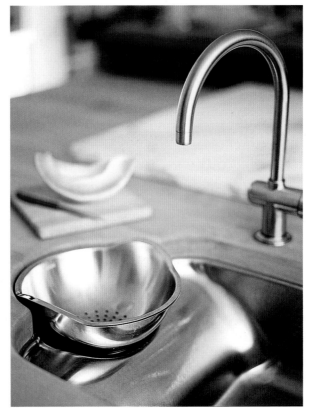

← **A CURVED COUNTERTOP CUTOUT** hugs the island's prep sink and integral colander.

EASY UPGRADE

Let your prep sink make a design statement with an unusual shape. They come round, square, rectangular, as narrow troughs (good for beverages when entertaining), even heart-shaped.

UNIFY THREE ROOMS

PROBLEM> The layout was workable, but the choice of materials was unappetizing.
SOLUTION> Cover the kitchen walls in floor-to-ceiling white tiles, add white cabinets, and inject a little drama with stainless steel and dark accents.

THESE DAYS MOST PEOPLE START A PROJECT by considering how little they can do—not how much—to transform a space. When the owners of this kitchen, with its red counters, blue-stained maple floor, and pickled cabinets, decided it was time for a redo, they dreamed of starting fresh in the nearby sunroom. Then cooler heads prevailed—their architect's among them. Together, the trio embarked on a dramatic but cosmetic update of the kitchen, continuing the same finishes in the adjacent breakfast room and pantry so that the three spaces worked as one. Materials were chosen for their light-reflecting qualities: white subway tile and cabinets, Carrara marble counters, and lots of stainless steel. The result is an updated yet traditional feel.

Proof positive of the project's success came when the owners had to move for a job change. "We told some friends the news," says the husband. "They immediately asked, 'Can we have the house?'" Today, the new owners and their three kids are enjoying the fruits of their friends' remodel. "The kitchen sold us," says the couple. "It's the one room where all five of us want to spend time."

White tile and cabinets, dark-stained floors, and lots of stainless steel give the space a new look and feel.

after

Open shelves allow natural light to bounce off the white-tile walls and marble counters. ↓

Scuff-resistant stainless-steel toekicks add → another touch of sheen.

Beveled subway tile on the walls and wainscot unites the cooking and eating spaces.
↓

↑COOL-HUED STAINLESS STEEL on the sink and range visually links the kitchen to the breakfast room with its icy blue walls.

the plan

BEFORE + AFTER
A stylistic update united the kitchen, breakfast room, and pantry, adding storage, light, and prep space—without altering the footprint or moving plumbing lines.

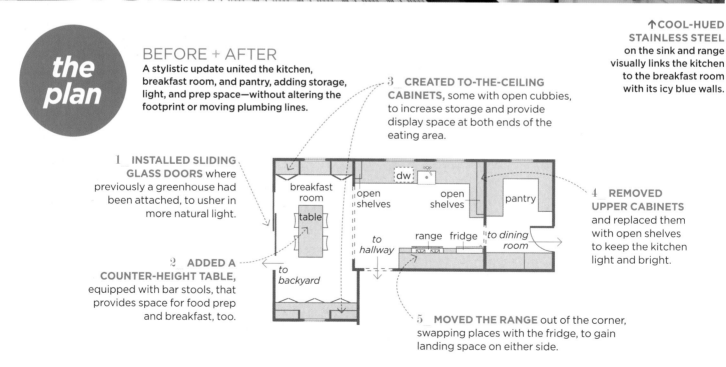

1 **INSTALLED SLIDING GLASS DOORS** where previously a greenhouse had been attached, to usher in more natural light.

2 **ADDED A COUNTER-HEIGHT TABLE,** equipped with bar stools, that provides space for food prep and breakfast, too.

3 **CREATED TO-THE-CEILING CABINETS,** some with open cubbies, to increase storage and provide display space at both ends of the eating area.

4 **REMOVED UPPER CABINETS** and replaced them with open shelves to keep the kitchen light and bright.

5 **MOVED THE RANGE** out of the corner, swapping places with the fridge, to gain landing space on either side.

Floor plan labels: breakfast room · table · to backyard · open shelves · dw · open shelves · pantry · to hallway · range · fridge · to dining room

the details

↓ **SLEEK OPEN SHELVES** were made by mortising inexpensive steel brackets into stained maple planks.

← **A MARBLE-TOPPED TABLE,** built by a local furniture maker, matches the counters. Its raised height, shelves, and slide-out cutting boards allow it to double as a prep island.

EASY UPGRADE

Give a worn wood floor a fresh, modern look with a dark stain. It will also hide repairs and patches better than a lighter tone.

→ **A DEEP FARMHOUSE SINK** in stainless steel reinforces the updated traditional style of the space and hides dirty dishes.

→ **A WIDE RANGE HOOD** delineates the cooking area. Bar pulls on appliances and drawers double as towel bars.

↑ **WINDOW SASHES** were painted glossy black to echo the floor stain. The contrast they provide helps ground the gleaming white walls. Even the metal window lifts coordinate with the other hardware in the room.

A shelf on the backsplash above the range keeps spices at the ready. →

The dimly lit kitchen lacked function as well as period charm.

after

Everything's new but looks old, from the cabinets' flat panels to the vintage-green wall tile to the schoolhouse lights.

FINESSE THE FRIDGE

PROBLEM> The boxy kitchen was big enough but lacked prep and storage space.
SOLUTION> Tweak the floor plan to get a larger work space, then introduce all-new finishes to get a fresh yet old-fashioned feel with lots more function.

SOMETIMES LIVING WITH A DYSFUNCTIONAL, dated space for years allows you to really envision the look and utility you want. When the owners got ready to overhaul the eat-in kitchen in this 1918 house, they yearned for a more period-appropriate style along with more storage and prep space—not to mention a 36-inch range and a 42-inch fridge. But they liked the room's proportions and saw no reason to make it bigger. After three years of pondering ways to squeeze more style and function into the existing footprint, they turned to a local designer to wring maximum benefit out of minimum rebuilding.

Casting about, the designer saw a way to cut into the back of a closet in an adjacent room and annex 6 square feet. "That let us have our fridge," says the wife. Then the designer helped the couple infuse the room with period detail and boost its efficiency, swapping out windows, reinstalling an original corner cabinet, and "tempering old with new," as she puts it, by blending vintage-look cabinets, tile, and lighting with sleek stainless-steel appliances. Says the husband, "We love our range—we use the built-in griddle for breakfast, lunch, and dinner." Classic white cabinets, enlivened by a pale-green tile backsplash and green walls, brighten the previously dark space. "Now it's a pleasure to cook," the wife adds. "And I can't tell you how many people say the new kitchen looks like it has always been there."

THE MOSTLY WHITE KITCHEN
> FINESSE THE FRIDGE

→ **A HANDY NEW** prep space has a tray cabinet to the left of the wine cooler, a glossy tile backsplash, and a pro-style stainless-steel countertop.

↓ **THE HEX-TILE FLOOR** unites the cooking area and a dining nook where the family likes to gather. Pale green walls visually connect the nook to the kitchen and its green backsplash.

Cabinet doors with glass inserts showcase collectibles while hiding clutter.

the plan

AFTER
Annexing a portion of the living room closet enabled the homeowners to squeeze in a large fridge, a longer run of countertop, and extra cabinets.

3 MOVED THE RANGE to the left to create more usable prep and landing space.

1 RELOCATED THE FRIDGE to create space for extra cabinets and spots for the wine cooler and above-counter microwave.

2 ANNEXED A FEW FEET from a closet to make room for the 42-inch fridge and adjacent counter space.

BEFORE
The kitchen was big enough for a table but lacked prep and storage space.

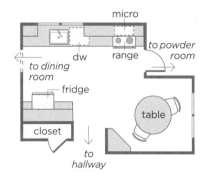

micro
dw
range
to powder room
to dining room
fridge
table
closet
to hallway

wine cooler
micro fridge
corner cupboard
dw range
to powder room
to dining room
table
closet
to living room

the details

↓ **THE ORIGINAL CORNER CUPBOARD,** removed during the construction phase, went back into its spot with a fresh coat of paint and new satin-nickel pulls.

A black-slate border unifies the irregular contours of the tile floor. →

↑ **FURNITURE-LIKE PILASTERS** and curved "feet" appear to support the farmhouse sink.

← **PORCELAIN HEXAGONAL TILE,** accented with a widely spaced flower motif and a black slate border, then finished with tan grout, enhances the kitchen's vintage look.

← **FLAT-PANEL INSET DOORS** and polished-nickel latches give the cabinets practical, old-fashioned appeal.

✱ TOH DESIGN ADVICE

Use white-on-white materials for an unbroken visual effect that makes any room feel larger.

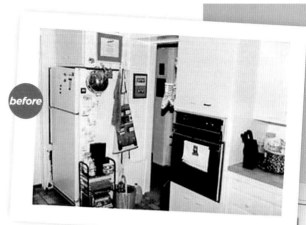

The long, narrow kitchen had few counters, bad workspace, and poor circulation.

before

FIND A NEW FOOTPRINT

PROBLEM> **A narrow galley kitchen with doors on two sides was crowded by frequent traffic jams.** SOLUTION> **Relocate the cook space to a first-floor bedroom and line all four walls with white.**

WHEN THE EMPHASIS OF A KITCHEN REMODEL is handsome practicality, the room can work hard for years without looking out of sync with the times. That's what the wife who cooks in this space envisioned, having endured a badly planned galley for years. The 1940 house that she shares with her husband and their two sons was built as a one-story weekend place not meant for serious cooking. Needing more room overall, they asked a local architect to add a second story and a kitchen that would be clean and simple and that they would still love in 30 years.

His first move was to relocate the bedrooms upstairs and turn the old galley into stairs, a sitting nook, and a powder room. The easiest part of the project was tucking the new kitchen and an adjacent breakfast area into the footprint of the old guest suite. Efficient and well proportioned, the new space has an island and loads of marble countertops. The cabinets are a model of organization, with each designated for specific items, such as cereal boxes or food-storage containers. Highly functional but warm, with cheerful green and yellow accents, the white kitchen has a timeless style that will stay fresh for years to come.

The new room is an efficient square with lots of food-prep and cleanup space, as well as plenty of storage.

after

A 2-by-9-foot skylight above a trio of windows brightens the space. →

→ TROPICAL-HARDWOOD FLOORING unifies the kitchen with the adjoining family room.

↓ DIAGONAL SHELVES for short-term wine storage make clever use of a sliver of space.

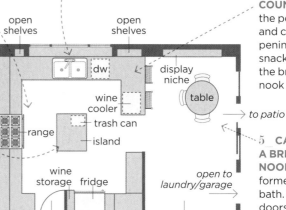

the plan

AFTER
Relocating the kitchen during a ground-floor reorganization yielded an ultra-functional, square-shaped workspace.

3 INSTALLED A SKYLIGHT (not shown) above a trio of windows, made possible by a small setback on the new second floor.

4 BUILT COUNTERS along the perimeter and created a peninsula with a snack counter on the breakfast-nook side.

1 MOVED THE KITCHEN to what had been a ground-floor guest bedroom. The architect kept the room's original footprint.

2 ADDED AN ISLAND with utensil drawers and a slide-out trash can. The new workspace has no door to the outside, so traffic flows around the island, not through the room.

5 CARVED A BREAKFAST NOOK out of the former guest bath. Sliding glass doors replaced small windows, providing access to the garden and bringing in light.

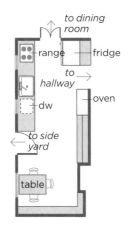

open shelves • open shelves • dw • display niche • table • to patio • wine cooler • trash can • island • range • wine storage • fridge • open to laundry/garage • open to family room • to family room

BEFORE
The galley was cramped and poorly organized, with an exterior door that invited traffic—and traffic jams.

to dining room • range • fridge • to hallway • dw • oven • to side yard • table

the details

→ **THE BREAKFAST NOOK,** where the family eats most meals, is out of the meal-prep area and has sliding glass doors leading to the patio and garden. A large niche was carved out of a wall next to the table as a space for rotating displays of decorative objects. The yellow-and-green theme helps bring the outdoors in.

← **A WINE COOLER** is tucked under the kitchen side of the peninsula. With the built-in bottle rack alongside the refrigerator, it helps make entertaining easy.

EASY UPGRADE

Use cabinet doors to cap an end run of cabinets or a peninsula for a more polished, paneled look.

↑ **SHELVES FOR PLATES AND CUPS** are within reach of the dishwasher. The owners chose a showy brown marble for the counters, which balances the look of the wood floors in the white room. It has a honed finish, rather than a polished one, for a softer look.

✳ TOH DESIGN ADVICE

Add open display shelves to personalize a kitchen. Recess them into niches for a clean, built-in look.

CHAPTER 10

MATERIALS GUIDE

How you outfit your kitchen—what you choose for your cabinets, countertops, faucet—will affect not only how well the room functions but also your enjoyment of it over the long haul. Shopping for materials is also one of the creative, fun parts of upgrading your space: checking out the options, discovering what you like, and seeing how it all fits into your plan (and budget). So before you hit the home center or start to search online, take a look at the following pages and some of the most popular options to consider.

1_ **Cabinets**

2_ **Sinks**

3_ **Faucets**

4_ **Countertops**

5_ **Backsplash**

5_ **Flooring**

>CABINETS

ALL KITCHEN CABINETS NEED replacing eventually. Whether they're falling apart after years of hard use or standing in the way of that work-triangle overhaul you've been planning, a coat of paint or new wood doors simply can't always save them.

With so many door styles, finishes, and interior organizers to choose from, such as built-in spice racks and pull-out pantries, ordering new cabinets is an exciting part of the process. But with a lot of money at stake—cabinets account for about half the cost of a typical kitchen renovation—it can also be daunting. To get the most bang for your buck, it's important to focus not just on good looks but also on quality of materials, types of hinges and other hardware, and the joinery that holds cabinets together. Those features determine whether your cabinets will keep your affections for the long haul or force you to start shopping again way too soon.

On the following pages, you'll find an overview of kitchen cabinets based on their construction, style, and price. Use it as a guide to help you figure out what you like and what you need as you begin to make your decisions. Once the new cabinets are in place, you'll wonder how you managed to live so long with the old ones.

Anatomy of a cabinet

With the exception of drawers and a toekick, upper and lower cabinets share the same basic elements.

CORNER BRACES
Keep carcass square during transport and installation.

CARCASS
Cabinet box; supports weight of countertop and items on shelves.

FACE FRAME
Stiles and rails that stiffen the carcass and provide a mount for hinges. (Not present with full overlay doors.)

DRAWER
Moves on metal glides fitted to the sides or bottom.

DOOR
Can have flat-panel, raised-panel, or slab fronts.

HINGE
Can be visible or hidden, depending on door type.

TOEKICK
Closes gap at cabinet base and provides a recess for feet.

door types

Doors come in dozens of different styles, but they're all just variations on a few basic forms.

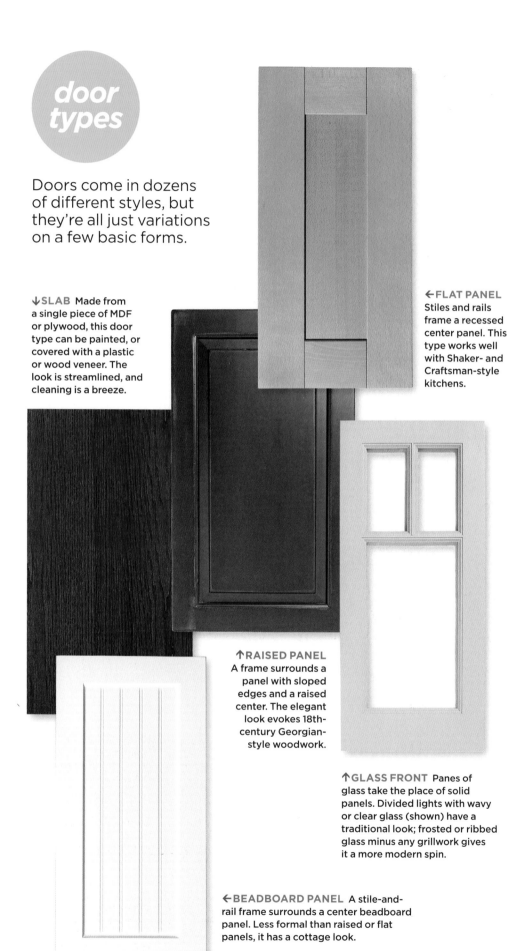

↓SLAB Made from a single piece of MDF or plywood, this door type can be painted, or covered with a plastic or wood veneer. The look is streamlined, and cleaning is a breeze.

←FLAT PANEL Stiles and rails frame a recessed center panel. This type works well with Shaker- and Craftsman-style kitchens.

↑RAISED PANEL A frame surrounds a panel with sloped edges and a raised center. The elegant look evokes 18th-century Georgian-style woodwork.

↑GLASS FRONT Panes of glass take the place of solid panels. Divided lights with wavy or clear glass (shown) have a traditional look; frosted or ribbed glass minus any grillwork gives it a more modern spin.

←BEADBOARD PANEL A stile-and-rail frame surrounds a center beadboard panel. Less formal than raised or flat panels, it has a cottage look.

Door and drawer mounting options

1_ Full overlay. Doors and drawer fronts completely cover the front of the cabinet, no face frame required. Uses concealed hinges, which can be easily adjusted.

2_ Inset. Doors fit perfectly flush with the face frame. Typically uses exposed hinges, but also works with concealed and surface-mount hinges.

3_ Partial overlay. Doors cover just a portion of the face frame. Uses concealed hinges. Doors that have a rabbet, or notch, cut into the outside edge so that only a thin lip overlies the face frame are called partial-inset.

Cabinetry guidelines

While cabinets can be configured in myriad ways, they're typically built and installed using well-established dimensions. Follow these rules of thumb during the planning stages to help you accurately imagine how your cabinets will look and function.

Distance between countertop and upper cabinets: 18 inches

Upper cabinet depth: 12 inches

Lower cabinet depth: 24 inches

Countertop overhang: ¾ to 1 inch

Toekick: 4 inches high, 3 inches deep

Countertop height: 36 inches

TOH DESIGN ADVICE

When planning your cabinetry, take into account not only what you'll store but also appliance location and traffic patterns so you have adequate clearance.

STOCK, SEMI-CUSTOM, OR CUSTOM?

The more a cabinet can be tailored to fit your kitchen and the beefier its construction, the higher the price. Stock comes in a limited range of sizes, semi-custom expands that choice, and custom is built to fit exact specifications.

	stock	**semi-custom**	**custom**
GOOD FOR	Tight budgets and fast turnarounds; some require assembly. Limited selection of styles, configurations, and finishes. Gaps can be bridged with filler strips.	More discriminating tastes and deeper pockets. Get any style, finish, or configuration, as long as it is in the manufacturer's catalog.	Kitchens where a precise fit, more configuration options, and fine detailing matter more than the price tag.
SIZES	Widths for uppers and lowers change in 3-inch increments. Heights vary in 6-inch increments on uppers; lowers are fixed.	Widths for uppers and lowers usually change in 1-inch increments. Heights vary in 6-inch increments on uppers; lowers are fixed.	Built to any width or height you want and with any finish, hardware, or wood type that catches your fancy.
MATERIALS, HARDWARE	Carcasses are typically ½-inch MDF (medium-density fiberboard) or particleboard sheathed in melamine. Doors are usually MDF covered in thermofoil or wood veneer. Drawer glides tend to be lightweight metal and don't allow the drawer to fully extend.	Carcasses are typically ½-inch MDF but often can be upgraded to plywood. Doors can be solid wood or MDF with thermofoil or wood veneer. Full-extension drawer glides are side-mounted.	Typically ¾-inch furniture-grade plywood for the carcasses; door and drawer fronts are usually solid wood. Full-extension glides can be undermounted and have a soft-close feature.
BUY THEM FROM	Home centers and big-box retailers. Allow one to five weeks for delivery.	Home centers or kitchen showrooms. Allow five to six weeks for delivery.	Kitchen showrooms or local cabinetmakers. Allow eight to 10 weeks for domestic cabinet delivery, 14 to 16 weeks for imports, and eight weeks to six months for a cabinetmaker.

Under-cabinet lighting

Ceiling and pendant fixtures are often as much about looks as they are about light, but under-cabinet lighting does its job discreetly. A workhorse in the kitchen, it provides task light over otherwise shadowy surfaces along a stretch of countertop. And while fixtures tucked under a run of cabinets can have an overall brightening effect in a room, their chief function is to light a work surface so that tasks such as cutting or chopping are performed safely and accurately.

There are three basic types to choose from. Strip lights, thanks to their linear shape, are good for reading a cookbook or working at a counter. Circular puck or disk lights cast pools of light where they are placed, so while they create a pleasing pattern of light and shadow, they are not ideal for tasks. Track systems consist of miniature lamps that snap onto a thin plastic channel and can be hidden by the smallest valance. Because they are moveable, lamps can be configured—and reconfigured—in a variety of ways.

Each fixture type offers different bulb options. Some require a transformer, so you need to allow room for that. Fluorescent is long-lasting but not generally dimmable. Halogen casts a crisp white light and can be dimmed, but it burns very hot, even when it is low voltage. Xenon is low voltage, cooler than halogen, and can be dimmed. Today, LED (light-emitting diode) is becoming the standard, as it is low voltage, cool, burns the longest, and is now affordable.

>SINKS

THE PRIMARY WORKSTATION in any kitchen is the sink. Consequently, the choice of bowl configuration and material becomes a highly individual preference. When planning an upgrade, go for tough materials and a big scale—a deeper, broader bowl and a higher spout on the faucet—for the most convenient set-up.

The debate over kitchen-sink materials centers on three key characteristics: durability, noise-dampening capacity, and ease of maintenance. Large sinks offer the option of one bowl or two. You may also have the opportunity to have more than one sink, placing a second in an island, peninsula, bar, or walk-in pantry. If you are lucky enough to have two, you may want to vary the size and have one large sink in the primary location with a smaller one in the secondary spot. Think about how you use your main sink throughout the day, for typical meal prep as well as cleanup and entertaining, and this will help you hone your selections.

↓DROP-IN This sink drops into a hole cut in the countertop for easy installation. The sink's rim supports its weight; caulking the perimeter keeps the seal watertight. The downside: Dirt can collect around the exposed rim.

←APRON FRONT Also referred to as a farmhouse sink, this sink is ideal for kitchens with a classic look. Typically made of fireclay or stone, the sink is recognizable by its broad panel front, which repels drips and splashes. Look for either an under-counter or a tile-in model, where the sink rim is level with the counter surface.

→UNDERMOUNT This attaches with clips to the underside of the counter for a seamless look that's easy to maintain. But because it leaves the countertop edge exposed to water, it can only be used with slab or molded materials, such as stone, solid surface, or concrete.

MATERIALS

STAINLESS STEEL Available in a full range of configurations, including an integrated drainboard. Stainless steel comes in many gauges: 16 is best. Higher-number gauges are thinner and sound "tinny." While it doesn't chip, stain, or rust, it can scratch.

FIRECLAY Typically used for apron-front sinks, this ceramic product is fired at an extremely high temperature for strength and durability. As with any ceramic, chipping is a danger. It has a high-gloss finish and is comparatively quiet.

ENAMELED CAST-IRON Available in a variety of configurations and colors, this material works well in a traditional kitchen. It can scratch or chip, and may break crockery that falls against it. Its heavy weight can lessen the din of a garbage disposer.

COMPOSITE A molded combination of quartz stone and acrylic polymer, this lightweight material holds color and resists fading, cuts, scratches, and stains. Mounted above or beneath the counter, it comes in many sizes and configurations.

SOLID SURFACE Can be integrated into a solid-surface countertop or mounted in countertops of other materials. A solid-surface sink is quiet, and minor stains and abrasions can be buffed out; otherwise care is the same as for countertops.

>FAUCETS

SELECT A SPOUT AND HANDLE STYLE based on what looks good with your cabinets. Also consider where it will be placed, the countertop material, and the size and shape of your sink. In picking a finish you'll want to take into account metal appliances and cabinet hardware so that everything is compatible. A satin finish helps minimize fingerprints. If your kitchen includes a second sink, you'll need to decide whether to match its faucet to the primary one or pick something that coordinates. Make sure any faucet has rugged, solid-brass construction and a drip-proof ceramic-disc valve, which is likely to last the longest, particularly if your water is hard or has lots of sediment. Here are the basic styles.

↓ STANDARD This classic design projects almost straight out from the deck for easy maintenance and a clean appearance. While it can handle most pots, it will not clear oversize ones easily. If you routinely cook with large-scale equipment, look for another style.

↓ GOOSENECK This graceful faucet, with its high arc, offers versatility by accommodating large items, such as roasting pans or pasta pots. It can be charmingly traditional or sleek and modern, and all handle and stem options are available, from dual- or single-control to bridge.

→ PULL-OUT A pull-out spray model cuts back on splashing and is convenient for tasks such as filling large pots, rinsing vegetables, or even bathing a small pet, because it extends the faucet's reach.

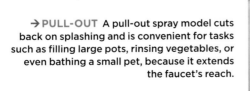

← PULL-DOWN
The spray head on this faucet pulls down from a high-arc spout, offering more height and reach than standard pull-out faucets. The head moves on a flexible hose, so water can be aimed precisely where you want it.

Handle choices

More than just a feature to control water temperature and flow, handles also play a part in your comfort and safety at the sink. Paying attention to how you and others use the sink will help you zero in on the right choice.

1_ Single control. One easy-to-use lever regulates both temperature and volume for quick and precise control of both. It also lets you keep one hand free. The lever design is rendered in both contemporary and traditional styles.

2_ Two handles. These models come with cross handles, levers, or knobs. Cross handles are practical in households with children, as they are easy for small, wet hands to manipulate.

3_ Wrist blades. Although wrist blades can have a traditional look, their main asset is functionality: They are the easiest to operate of all handle styles, making them appropriate for those with limited manual dexterity.

→ PRO-STYLE OR POT-WASHER
Inspired by faucets found in restaurant kitchens, this oversize spigot has a big reach and a spot for docking. Its 140-degree swivel makes it easy to maneuver and a good partner for big double-bowl sinks that accommodate a lot of large cookware.

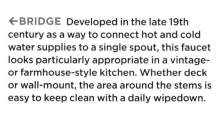

↑ HANDS-FREE Once solely for commercial use, this tap-on, water-saving device is now available for the home kitchen. It keeps the faucet germ-free when you are handling raw food or dirty dishes. Manual controls let you preset the water temperature and the faucet stream's shutoff time.

← BRIDGE Developed in the late 19th century as a way to connect hot and cold water supplies to a single spout, this faucet looks particularly appropriate in a vintage- or farmhouse-style kitchen. Whether deck or wall-mount, the area around the stems is easy to keep clean with a daily wipedown.

>COUNTERTOPS

BASE YOUR SELECTION OF work surface on the tasks and activities you perform on it: prep, dining, entertaining, baking. Looks matter too, of course, and you can get a custom effect from mixing materials—even in the same spot, such as an island that's half wood and half stone. Since the kitchen is a wet area, make sure any selection is waterproof. All materials show wear eventually; for care, follow the manufacturer's instructions. Here, the most popular options to consider.

1_NATURAL STONE This category includes granite, marble, limestone, slate, and soapstone, each in a range of colors and finishes. Slabs come in 4- to 8-foot lengths. Be aware that joints may show. Some stone, such as marble, is quite porous. Ask if sealing is recommended, and how often.

2_SOLID SURFACE A nonporous plastic-and-mineral composite, this material is "renewable," meaning small scratches and stains can be buffed out. Choices include stone lookalikes as well as rainbow colors. It is seamless, can be given a matte or high-gloss finish, and doesn't require sealing.

3_LAMINATE A veneer (plastic or metal) bonded to a particleboard substrate, laminate offers an easy-clean surface. It is also vulnerable to heat, scratches, burns, and water at its seams, so stick to drop-in sinks that cover the edges of the substrate.

4_ENGINEERED STONE A mix of 93 percent quartz granules held together with a resin binder, this man-made stone combines the ruggedness of granite with the color choices of solid surface. It does not require sealing.

5_CONCRETE Highly adaptable, concrete can take almost any shape, finish, and color. Though rugged and heat resistant, it needs sealing. Since it is fabricated with holes for fixtures, you must choose a sink and faucet first.

6_BUTCHER BLOCK Hardwood strips (usually maple, beech, or oak) cut into even or varying lengths are glued, then laminated under pressure to make butcher block. Can be oiled or sealed; forgo the latter if you plan to cut on it.

>BACKSPLASH

THE VERTICAL SURFACE just above the countertop can be painted or papered, of course. But more often it is protected with a durable, easy-to-maintain material that safeguards against spills and spatters. Since it is not a work surface, the backsplash can be treated with a wide range of decorative options. It is a good place for a splurge, too, especially behind the stove where you can create an eye-catching focal point for relatively little investment. No need to sacrifice performance for looks, either: All of the options featured here are as practical as they are pretty to behold.

↓ **TILE** This material continues to be a top choice as it offers the greatest potential for customization without stretching your budget. Even fragile art tiles and relief designs work beautifully on a vertical surface. Take care to seal grout lines against staining.

↓ **SOLID-SURFACE** Use a ½-inch-thick version, which is lighter than the standard countertop and thus easier to attach. If the countertop is also solid surface, consider an integral "cove" backsplash. For decorative effect, try an inlay in a contrasting color.

→ **BEADBOARD** In vintage-style kitchens, painted or stained beadboard provides an integrated look. Scrubbable, enamel-finish paints are most durable. Stained beadboard should get a polyurethane top coat for easy cleaning.

↑ **METAL** A solid stainless-steel backsplash is handsome but pricey. Alternatives are metal laminates and veneers, thin metal sheets adhered to a substrate, available as sheets or tiles. They can be made of stainless steel, copper, brass, or aluminum, and can be stamped with decorative designs.

>FLOORING

CONSTANT, HEAVY USE IS THE rule of the day for kitchen floors. So, carefully consider durability and upkeep when evaluating different materials—but factor in comfort, safety, and style too. Don't forget to calculate installation costs, which vary widely. Flooring is generally laid before the cabinetry, so it will need to be protected while the rest of your project is completed. Here are some popular options.

1_ **WOOD** While the kitchen is a wet area, wood remains highly desirable there due to its quiet properties and classic looks. Sealed floors should be maintained with a daily dry mop to eliminate grit that can dull the finish.

2_ **LAMINATE** A decorative paper layer (a photo image of wood grain, stone, or tile) is supported by an engineered-wood base and topped with a protective wear coat. The floor is relatively resilient and quiet, but vulnerable to standing water.

3_ **RESILIENT FLOORING** The most common type, vinyl, comes sandwiched between a cushioning base layer and a protective top coat. An all-natural alternative is linoleum (shown), made from cork, tree resin, and linseed oil. Both come as a sheet, click-together planks, or tiles and are easy underfoot, low maintenance, and muffle noise.

4_ **PORCELAIN TILE** Stronger than ceramic, porcelain is the floor tile of choice and comes in a wide array of styles, including faux wood. Its hardness makes it durable, but not the best choice if you are on your feet for long periods or have small children who take spills.

5_ **CORK** This cushiony surface can be laid as a sheet, tiles, or click-together planks and is appreciated for its comfort, warmth, and quiet. It generally comes stained in a range of colors and coated for easier cleaning.

6_ **BAMBOO** This hard, water-resistant floor (made from a grass, not a wood) comes prefinished, or unfinished to be stained to your specifications. Planks can be nailed or glued to a subfloor or laid as a floating floor.

>INDEX

>CREDITS

Front Cover: Photograph: Nathan Kirkman

Back Cover: Photographs: (left to right) Stephen Karlisch; Richard Leo Johnson; J. Curtis

p. 1: Photographs: (left to right) Eric Roth; Jason Varney; Mark Lohman

p. 2: Photographs: (left to right) Alex Hayden; Aimee Herring; Susan Gilmore

p. 3: Photographs: (left to right) Wendell T. Webber; John Ellis; J. Curtis

pp. 6–9: Illustrations: Arthur Mount

p. 11: Photograph: Julian Wass

pp. 12–15: Photographs: Eric Roth. Illustrations: Ian Worpole

pp. 16–19: Photographs: David Fenton. Illustrations: Ian Worpole

pp. 20–23: Photographs: Nathan Kirkman. Illustrations: Ian Worpole

pp. 25–27: Photographs: Alex Hayden. Illustrations: Ian Worpole

pp. 28–31: Photographs: Nathan Kirkman. Illustrations: Ian Worpole

p. 33: Photograph: Richard Leo Johnson

pp. 34–37: Photographs: Jürgen Frank. Illustration: Ian Worpole

pp. 38–41: Photographs: John Granen. Illustration: Ian Worpole

pp. 42–45: Photographs: Mark Lohman. Illustrations: Ian Worpole

p. 46: Photograph: Deborah Whitlaw Llewellyn

p. 47: Photographs: (top) J. Savage Gibson; (bottom) Deborah Whitlaw Llewellyn

p. 48: Photographs: (top) Mark Samu; (bottom) Laurey W. Glenn

p. 49: Photographs: (top) Tria Giovan; (bottom) Deborah Whitlaw Llewellyn

p. 50: Photograph: Colin Poole/IPC Images

p. 51: Photographs: (clockwise from top left) Christopher Drake/Loupe Images; Eric Roth; Jack Thompson; Dominique Vorillon; Deborah Whitlaw Llewellyn; Christopher Drake/Loupe Images

p. 53: Photograph: Deborah Whitlaw Llewellyn

pp. 54–57: Photographs: Jack Thompson. Illustrations: Ian Worpole

pp. 58–61: Photographs: John Ellis. Illustrations: Ian Worpole

p. 63: Photograph: Laura Moss

p 64: Photographs: (left) Tom McWilliam; (right) Laura Moss. Illustration: Ian Worpole

p. 65: Photographs: (clockwise from top left) Tom McWilliam (3); Laura Moss

pp. 66–69: Photographs: David Carmack. Illustrations: Ian Worpole

pp. 70–73: Photographs: Nathan Kirkman. Illustrations: Ian Worpole

pp. 74–77: Photographs: Jürgen Frank. Illustrations: Ian Worpole

pp. 78–81: Photographs: Janis Nicolay. Illustrations: Ian Worpole

p. 83: Photograph: Laurey W. Glenn

pp. 84–87: Photographs: Eric Piasecki. Illustrations: Ian Worpole

pp. 89–91: Photographs: David Fenton. Illustrations: Ian Worpole

pp. 93–95: Photographs: Joe Schmelzer. Illustrations: Ian Worpole

p. 97: Photograph: Laura Moss

pp. 99–101: Photographs: Mark Lohman. Illustration: Ian Worpole

pp. 103–105: Photographs: Gregg Segal. Illustrations: Ian Worpole

pp. 106–109: Photographs: Julian Wass. Illustrations: Ian Worpole

pp. 110–113: Photographs: Jason Varney. Illustrations: Ian Worpole

pp. 114–117: Photographs: Nathan Kirkman. Illustrations: Ian Worpole

p. 118: Photograph: John Granen

p. 119: Photographs: (clockwise from top) Alex Hayden; Tria Giovan; Walt Roycraft

p. 120: Photographs: (left) Nikki Crisp/IPC Images; (right) Nathan Kirkman

p. 121: Photographs: (top) Stephen Karlisch; (bottom) Deborah Whitlaw Llewellyn

p. 122: Photograph: Dana Gallagher

p. 123: Photographs: (top) Matthew Millman; (bottom) Bob Narod

p. 125: Photograph: Deborah Whitlaw Llewellyn

pp. 126–129: Photographs: Matthew Millman. Illustrations: Ian Worpole

pp. 130–133: Photographs: Pascal Blancon. Illustrations: Ian Worpole

pp. 135–137: Photographs: David Prince. Illustrations: Ian Worpole

p. 139: Photograph: Wendell T. Webber

pp. 141–143: Photographs: David Prince. Illustration: Ian Worpole

pp. 145–147: Photographs: Andrea Rugg. Illustrations: Ian Worpole

pp. 149–151: Photographs: J. Curtis. Illustrations: Ian Worpole

pp. 152–155: Photographs: Eric Piasecki

p. 157: Photograph: Thomas J. Story

pp. 158–161: Photographs: Michael Jensen. Illustrations: Ian Worpole

pp. 162–165: Photographs: Alise O'Brien. Illustration: Ian Worpole

pp. 166–169: Photographs: Andrew Bordwin. Illustrations: Ian Worpole

p. 171: Photograph: Alexandra Rowley

pp. 172–175: Photographs: Wendell T. Webber. Illustrations: Ian Worpole

pp. 177–179: Photographs: Aimee Herring. Illustrations: Ian Worpole

pp. 180–183: Photographs: Susan Gilmore. Illustration: Ian Worpole

pp. 184–187: Photographs: Paul Whicheloe. Illustrations: Ian Worpole

pp. 188–191: Photographs: Mark Lohman. Illustrations: Ian Worpole

p. 193: Photograph: Yunhee Kim

p. 194: Photograph: Karen Melvin. Illustration: Rodica Prato

p. 195: Photographs: ("Door Types") Don Penny/Time Inc. Digital Studio

p. 196: Photograph: Matthew Millman

p. 198: Photograph: (top) Alex Hayden

p. 201: Photographs: ("Natural Stone") Mark Lohman; ("Concrete") Kristine Larsen; ("Butcher Block") Susan Seubert

p. 202: Photographs: ("Tile") Michael Luppino; ("Beadboard") Stephen Karlisch

p. 203: Photographs: ("Wood") Julian Wass; ("Porcelain Tile") David Prince; ("Cork") Kolin Smith; ("Bamboo") Jürgen Frank

p. 205: Photograph: Laurey W. Glenn

p. 208: Photograph: Don Penny/Time Inc. Digital Studio

©2011 by Time Home Entertainment Inc.
135 West 50th Street
New York, NY 10020

ISBN-10: 0-8487-3472-6
ISBN-13: 978-0-8487-3472-5
Library of Congress Control Number: 2011929378

Printed in the United States of America
First Printing 2011

To order additional publications,
call 1-800-765-6400 or 1-800-491-0551.

For more books to enrich your life, visit oxmoorhouse.com.

To subscribe to *This Old House* magazine, go to thisoldhouse.com/customerservice or call 1-800-898-7237.

31901050903436